Feed My Sheep

A Commentary on 1 & 2 Peter

William VanDoodewaard

EP BOOKS
(Evangelical Press) Registered Office: 140 Coniscliffe Road, Darlington, Co Durham DL3 7RT

www.epbooks.org
admin@epbooks.org

EP Books are distributed in the USA by:
JPL Books, 3883 Linden Ave. S.E.,
Wyoming, MI 49548

www.jplbooks.com
orders@jplbooks.com

First published 2017

British Library Cataloguing in Publication Data available

ISBN 978-1-78397-191-6

Contents

Preface

This volume is dedicated to my wife, Rebecca, and children, Anna, Matthew, Julia, and Louisa, along with all of the dear saints from Holy Trinity Presbyterian Church, who patiently and prayerfully encouraged me as a fellow servant, elder, and minister of the Lord Jesus Christ, from the inception of the congregation through 2016. They taught me much both in cheerful thankfulness in prosperity, and in looking to Jesus, their Good Shepherd, as they suffered trials and afflictions. I am deeply grateful to the Lord for that precious season of co-laboring for Christ. It is my prayer that the Lord will bless this volume along with the many other good fruits his people bear, as he continues to build his church.

My thanks are also due to Graham Hind and the patient staff at Evangelical Press who enabled this manuscript to come to press, as well as to Puritan Reformed Theological Seminary for giving space for writing as a part of my vocation. Above all I am thankful to our Triune God for His steadfast mercy, grace, and love.

An Introduction to the Epistles of Peter

Peter, a servant and apostle

The opening verses of both first and second Peter declare the human authorship of these epistles: it is Peter, Simon Peter, a servant and an apostle of Jesus Christ. (cf. 2 Peter 1:1) Who is this man, chosen and inspired by God to pen these letters? As we turn to the New Testament we gain a substantial view of Peter: an ordinary man, saved and sanctified by Jesus to a new life of kingdom service.

We first encounter Peter in the divine record when his brother Andrew, hearing John the Baptist proclaim that Jesus is "the Lamb of God", tells Peter about Jesus. "We have found the Messiah", he says, bringing Peter to Jesus. Jesus recognizes him as "Simon the son of John" and declares that his name will be "Cephas" in Aramaic, or Peter in Greek, meaning "rock" (John 1:35–42). The next time we meet Peter is on the shore of the Sea of Galilee, engaged in his fishing trade, working with his brother on the boat. This is when Jesus calls them both: "follow me, I will make you fishers of men" (Matthew 4:18–20). In his years as a disciple, the Galilean fisherman often seems anything but a sturdy rock. He is impetuous, quick to speak, and prone to trouble. When Jesus walks on the water, Peter is excited to try, too, but quickly fails (Matthew 14:25–33). But there are also moments when God's grace shines through Peter in a strong faith. When Jesus, aware of the rumors, asks the disciples, "who do you say that I am?" Peter's certain reply is, "you are the Christ, the Son of the living God" (Matthew 16:15). Yet, it is the same Peter who not long after seeks to dissuade Jesus from his atoning mission, receiving Christ's strong rebuke: "Get behind ME, Satan! You are a stumbling block to me; for you are not setting your mind on God's interests, but man's" (Matthew 16:21–23).

This back-and-forth pattern continues. When disciples desert Jesus in droves, he asks the twelve whether they will too. It is Peter who says "Lord to whom shall we go? You have the words of eternal life. We have believed and come to know that you are the Holy One of God" (John 6:66–69). Yet, on the few recorded times when Christ asks his disciples to persevere in prayer, Peter falls asleep. At the transfiguration, Peter blurts out the suggestion of making three tabernacles, one each for Jesus, Moses, and Elijah (Matthew 17:1–4; Luke 10:28–36). In the Garden of Gethsemane, on the evening of his assertion that he will never deny Jesus, Peter wakes up to the approaching mob, pulls out his sword and cleaves the ear off Malchus, the high priest's servant. Commanded by Christ to sheathe his sword, his courage ebbs away. After furtively following Jesus, he then falls into lying, repeatedly denying his Lord (Matthew 26; Mark 14; Luke 22). The rooster crows, and catching Jesus' gaze, Peter leaves and weeps bitterly.

We see Peter again among the first disciples to hear of the empty tomb from Mary Magdalene. He goes to see and is full of wonder. Despite meeting the risen Christ in the locked room with the other disciples, Peter continues in uncertainty and spiritual disarray (John 20). No doubt still feeling the weight of his recent denial, he returns to fishing. After a miserable night, Jesus arrives on shore unrecognized and instructs them to fish on the other side of the boat, with incredible results. Suddenly aware of his Lord, Peter jumps into the water to get to shore faster. Here, after sharing breakfast, Jesus questions Peter's love, probes the sincerity of his heart, calling him to "feed my sheep" and once again "follow me," in gracious restoration (John 21).

The Peter we read of in the book of Acts is a transformed man. He has witnessed his Lord's ascension to glory (Acts 1). He is devoted to prayer with the others in the upper room and with them is filled with the Holy Spirit. In new boldness and power he proclaims the gospel of Jesus Christ in Jerusalem, the very city that had crucified his Lord only a few weeks earlier (Acts 2). Imprisonments and persecutions do not stop Peter from preaching—they become occasions for gospel proclamation. The Lord greatly uses him as an apostle to lead, shepherd, and feed the flock. Peter travels through Judea and Palestine, Syria, and into Asia Minor to expand and strengthen the church. Yet Peter is not without sin. He has to be rebuked by his fellow apostle, Paul, for cowing under the pressures of the Judaizers (Galatians 2). Despite this, the evidence of Christ's preserving and sanctifying grace at work in Peter is also evident—by the middle of the Jerusalem council held to discuss the relationship of the Gentile church to aspects of Jewish ceremony, he stands together with Paul for the cause of the gospel of Jesus Christ (Acts 15). While the divinely inspired record of Peter's life and ministry ends with the book of Acts and his epistles, the record of early church historians indicates that Peter followed the Savior unto death itself, dying as a martyr around AD 65.

A servant and apostle of Jesus Christ

In the opening verse of the first epistle, Peter describes himself not only by his name but as 'an apostle of Jesus Christ.' (1 Peter 1:1) The word "apostle" is found throughout the New Testament. In John 16:13, after washing the disciples' feet, Jesus proceeds to teach them that as messengers (apostles) they are servants. As servants of their Lord and Teacher, serving his kingdom as messengers bearing his Word, they have divinely designated authority. The use of the term "apostle" in the New Testament includes the dual aspects of a personal, immediate calling and sending by Jesus Christ as Redeemer and King, the head of the church.[1] So when Peter states this office, God declares to us that this is an eyewitness of Jesus Christ, his life, sufferings, death and resurrection. Peter is a man who is now 'a servant' (2 Peter 1:1) and a messenger of Christ. The rest of verse one reinforces this apostolic reality: 'of Jesus Christ.' Peter is a man like us: a sinner, saved by grace in Christ, experiencing the struggles and triumphs of Christian life. But Peter is bringing a message to the church, to us, from the Son of God, the Lord and Savior with whom he walked, talked, and whom he followed in his earthly ministry. Peter serves us by bringing this message, he serves as a messenger of Jesus, under his ascended, glorious, mediatorial kingship.

The reality and implication of this is astounding. It should quiet us in reverence and fill us with eager anticipation. Through a man who sinned miserably, Peter, a man saved by grace alone, rescued and transformed by Jesus, Christ speaks his Word to us. Does your heart thrill to these opening words? God is so gracious and good. Look at what he has done for Peter, and now for us through Peter. What a mystery of love and mercy! Praise God for his Word, for the privilege to listen and hear as he speaks to you.

The Audience

While it is valuable to know Peter, it is also valuable to understand the initial audience to whom the epistles were addressed. If we know that it is the Word of God "which remains forever," directly relevant to every generation, why bother with the original audience? Perhaps the best reason is that God tells us about them in his Word: he wants us to know. He cares for his church, and every individual member, in every generation.

The latter half of 1 Peter 1:1 gives us an immediate introduction to the first hearers of this part of God's Word. Peter addresses the first epistle to 'those who are elect exiles of the dispersion in Pontus, Galatia, Cappadocia, Asia, and Bithynia' (1 Peter 1:1).[2] His second epistle notes 'this is now the second letter I am writing to you' (2 Peter 3:1), so it is highly likely that both epistles were addressed to the same audience.[3] Peter's language indicates that he is addressing a people who are scattered through several regions or provinces of Asia Minor. The term Peter uses here was a common word referring to the dispersion of the Jews after the Assyrian and Babylonian period of exile. But as we read his epistles it is clear that Peter is addressing Gentile believers as well, particularly in light of the references to their conversion from pagan ways of life (cf. 1 Peter 1:18, 4:3–4). So why would Peter use this term for both Jewish and Gentile believers? It is because together they make up the church, and in comparison to the world around them, they are small in number, scattered through the world like seeds on a field. These early Christians, just like us, are strangers, aliens, pilgrims and exiles, belonging to another kingdom, not of this world. As Savior and King of his church, Jesus Christ reminds us here that he is our Good Shepherd: he knows us and our trials in this world. Charles Simeon writes, "contemptible as Christians often appear in the eyes of men, they are of high estimation in the sight of God."[4]

The Letters and their Context

When were these epistles of Peter written? Accepting their stated authorship, it is probable that Peter wrote them in the 60s, prior to the death of the emperor Nero (AD 68), a period where the church experienced a mixture of liberty and persecution. Early church writings tell us that Peter was martyred outside Rome during Nero's reign. Both of Peter's epistles make references to Paul's epistles, arguably including portions of his prison epistles, written between 61–63. From this it appears that Peter's letters were very likely written between the years 63 and 67. By this point, Peter is at least middle aged, with some 30 years having elapsed since Christ's death, resurrection, and ascension. Peter has proclaimed the gospel in Jerusalem, through Judea, Samaria, Syria, and possibly Greece (1 Corinthians 1:12; 3:22) and Asia Minor (1 Peter 1:1), travelling with his wife on missionary journeys (1 Corinthians 9:5). His second epistle bears the note of finality and impending departure: "I know that the putting off of my body will be soon, as our Lord Jesus Christ made clear to me" (2 Peter 1:14). And so, by inspiration of the Holy Spirit, Peter completes his part in recording for all ages Christ's Word to his people, making "every effort so that after my departure you may be able at any time to recall these things" (2 Peter 1:15).

The First Epistle of Peter: Hope and Holiness (1 Peter 1–5)

1

Sovereign Grace and Peace

Please read 1 Peter 1:1–2

Chosen by God (1:1)

'Peter, an apostle of Jesus Christ,' (1:1) states that this apostolic letter, as the Word of God, is addressed to Christians who live as aliens, scattered across Asia Minor. They are a people who feel the realities of being strangers in society; they are marked as different by their purpose, life direction, faith, hope, and godliness. They are set apart as belonging to a different society, a different kingdom. Peter, as Jesus Christ's messenger, assures them that the Triune God knows their situation. Jesus, God Incarnate, understands their situation and is coming to speak to them in it. Through Peter, he tends and feeds his sheep.

The way in which our Lord speaks through his servant here is wonderful. Tenderly addressing them in their circumstances, he now begins to open their eyes to glorious spiritual realities. Jesus wants his church—wants you—to know and remember who he is, what he has done, and is doing for his people. While they are scattered, suffering strangers in this world, and feel this acutely, there is a larger reality: they are his 'elect' (1:1).[1]

The word "elect" here is one form of a group of words that Scripture uses in contexts referring to the doctrine of election (cf. Matthew 22:14; 24:22–31; Romans 8:33; 2 Timothy 2:10). Sometimes we may balk at election or we may wrongly understand it. But it is not as though people are trying to crowd into heaven, and God is picking a few and saying no to the rest. The reality is that we are all rebelliously running headlong away from God, running to destruction and judgment. Election is God graciously reaching out and, in the mystery of his love, effectually taking hold of and retrieving some so that they willingly come to him.[2] In using the term "elect," Peter draws believers' attention to a glorious, mysterious, and deeply comforting reality: God speaks here to men, women, and children whom he has chosen out of a futile way of life (1 Peter 1:18, 4:1–3; cf. Romans 3:10–11; John 6:37; Ephesians 1:4–5, 2:4–5). In his sovereign love and powerful redemption, they are brought to salvation and new life in Christ. The elect are the objects of God's mercy and grace, selected from rebel humanity not because they were any better, not because God saw in advance that they were different than others or more willing to believe. No, it was the Triune God who in love and mercy worked in them both to will and to do His good pleasure (Philippians 2:13).

Triune comfort and purpose (1:2)

Verse two opens the idea of "elect" even more. Three phrases show us God's sovereign, saving choice of believers. The first of these is that the Christians addressed here as the scattered church of Asia Minor are elect 'according to the foreknowledge of God the Father.' (1:2) Peter tells us, "Christians, you are known and chosen by God the Father. God the Father has known you whom he purposed to redeem from all eternity—long before our created existence." By the Spirit, Peter tells us that our Creator, Sustainer, and Redeemer knows us intimately. Yet, no reason can be given for election apart from God's sovereign free love and perfect will. Alexander Nisbet says that the Father, "having all persons ... under his all-seeing eye ... did out of his free love condescend upon some in particular, while others were passed by."[3] He has mercy on whom he will have mercy and compassion on whom he will have compassion (Romans 9:17). We simply know that it is not because of anything good in us (cf. Ephesians 2:1–10; Romans 3). John Brown illustrates that this is the pattern declared across Scripture: "when the Lord set his love on Israel, and chose them to be his peculiar people, the cause was not in them, but in himself; it was just because he loved them ...."[4] The foreknowledge of God the Father is his choosing to love, knowing and loving in advance, simply because it is his delight to love his people.

Peter describes how the Father carries out this election in the second modifying phrase: 'in the sanctification of the Spirit.' (1:2) These scattered believers are chosen by the Spirit's sanctifying work. While we often think of the Spirit's sanctifying work in relation to our growth in holiness, Scripture also uses the term more broadly to refer to a "setting apart" or a spiritual separation. It describes the change from identification with a rebel world, to an identity in belonging to God, living a new life in and for Him.

Old Testament Israel was to be an illustration of what spiritual separation was; they were a people whom God had set apart. In the Old Testament era this separation was civic and national in part, but ultimately spiritual. In the New Testament era there is a glorious continuity and global expansion of this spiritual setting apart: God's elect are set apart to God by the work of the Holy Spirit, becoming strangers and pilgrims in this world.

As the gospel of the Lord Jesus Christ goes out to the ends of the earth, those on whom God has set his love, are transformed and set apart. By Christ's redemption accomplished and applied, believers are made different where there is no natural difference.

Connected to this "setting apart" work of the Holy Spirit is the third phrase that modifies what it means to be elect. To what are God's people chosen, or elected? They are chosen 'for obedience to Jesus Christ and for sprinkling with his blood.' (1:2) As a Christian, you, with God's people, have been chosen for obedience to Jesus Christ. This is really the result of the Holy Spirit's sanctifying work: by his regeneration, people come to faith in Christ and at the same time begin to obey Christ. Transformed by grace, they obey the gospel call and pursue a life of thankful obedience to God's whole law. A similar, though negative, use of the term "obey" is found in 2 Thessalonians 1:6–10 where Paul speaks of those, "who do not obey the gospel of our Lord Jesus Christ." Obedience is an inseparable fruit of faith. The very act of faith in believing the gospel reflects obedience (cf. Romans 6:17).

Peter states that believers are not only chosen to obey Christ, but also to "be sprinkled by his blood." These words bring to mind an image which would have been particularly vivid for the Jewish believer. In the Old Testament, God had ordained the ceremony of His people being sprinkled with the blood of the sacrifices which were the picture of the sealing of His covenant of grace with them. It was a picture of removal of the guilt and pollution of sin—a picture that, just like the Passover lamb, Jesus perfectly fulfilled as his hands and feet were pierced, his blood shed, while he took the full weight of God's wrath against the sin of his people.

When God selects individuals, sets them spiritually apart to be his people, and brings them to faith in the gospel, it is so that they gain personal inclusion in blessing in Christ, through his atoning sacrifice. Now their sins can be and are forgiven; their guilt can be and is removed. Christians are enabled and brought with a true heart to God and come to live in spiritual fellowship with him. God conforms the elect to his will: they now want the perfect good he wants and obedience becomes delightful and good to them. This is not only because he has made them, but because the precious blood of Christ has redeemed them[5] (1 Peter 1:18).

This, then, is the identity of the people of God declared by the Holy Spirit: you are those who belong to God, redeemed in Triune wisdom and love. It is as if Peter, Jesus' messenger, says, "Look at how God loves you. He knows your trials. Listen as he tells you his sovereign love; would he have chosen you, brought you to faith, and sprinkled you with the blood of his only begotten Son, if he were not willing to bless you today, tomorrow, and for all eternity?"

Grace and peace multiplied (1:2)

Then comes the Lord's blessing: 'grace and peace be multiplied to you.' (1:2) Grace is free favor, God's sovereign kindness. The New Testament often uses the word as a general term for all the blessings that flow from God's sovereign, saving love, including those that Peter just described. Peace is contentment and trust in God's wisdom, will, and power, received as we are restored to communion with God in Christ. Peter declares to the church, alien in the world, "May you have continued, increasing, multiple proofs that God loves you, in the continuing, increasing, the multiplying of His blessings. May you know that you are heirs with Christ, children of God, receiving a kingdom that cannot be shaken."

You and the Word

Do you feel that you are a stranger in the world, even as you live by faith? Have you felt the cold shoulder of co-workers, the distance of former friends, or separation from family members who are not in Christ? Do you feel the loneliness of ostracism or the pressures of outright persecution?

John Calvin, writing in the midst of the difficulties of the Reformation, said of this passage,

> all other things will be deemed worthless when we consider what Christ and his blessings are ... for this reason [Peter] highly extols the wonderful grace of God in Christ, that is that we may not deem it much to give up the world ... and that we may not be broken down by present troubles, but patiently endure them ...[6]

Listen to God as he speaks to you in these verses. He is telling his people how highly he esteems them. Doesn't it soothe and refresh your soul to hear the Lord remind you of his love at the cost of his Son's sufferings and death to bring you into a life of peace with him? Let the Lord put your present sufferings and struggles in this glorious context. Be glad, give thanks to God, praise him, rest in him: grace and peace be multiplied to you.

But if you have not experienced this, if your heart does not resonate with these words, then realize that his grace and peace, his eternal love can be yours by coming to Christ. His promise is simply, ask and you will receive, seek and you will find. Seek first his kingdom and his righteousness, and you and your need will be satisfied in him.

2

Sons of God

Please read 1 Peter 1:3–5

Gratitude for life (1:3)

Filled with the Word and the Spirit, Peter bursts into worship and praise of God the Father in verse 3: 'Blessed be the God and Father of our Lord Jesus Christ!' (1:3) Why is Peter's heart overflowing with praise? Because the Father, through Jesus Christ, has given new life and new status to Peter and all the believers whom he addresses. John Calvin comments that we are all "born children of wrath," yet 'according to his great mercy, he has caused us to be born again' (1:3). The Father rebirths us, by his Word and Spirit, in and through the person and work of His Son, victoriously displayed in his resurrection.[1]

The words "born again" are equivalent to those that Jesus speaks to Nicodemus in John 3:3 and 7.[2] In this context they carry with them both the idea of new life and the implication of sonship—we are "born" or "begotten" as a child of a biological parent. What a mystery God's Word declares here: the privilege of being rebirthed as the sons of God!

By natural conception and birth we are rebel creatures, strangers to and enemies of God's family. Romans 8:14–16 makes it clear that this Spirit-worked new birth in Christ not only brings us back into God's presence and fellowship, but also under his Fatherhood. We are transformed to become God's children, not only in status, but also in reality, so that we can cry out "Abba! Father!" (Romans 8:15). We receive all the rights and privileges of sonship. How has God accomplished this new birth, this sonship, for us? Peter tells us, 'the God and Father of our Lord Jesus Christ ... caused us to be born again ... through the resurrection of Jesus Christ from the dead' (1:3). Our new birth and new life as the children of God is because of Jesus' death and resurrection; this was not a cheap venture. It was supremely costly. You were bought with the price of the blood, the death, of the Son of God (1 Peter 1:19), Your redemption is sealed, made sure, in his resurrection.

Here, Peter brings us to see that God's mercy-filled power causes us to be born again, preserving us in new life as living, growing children of the Father. The same power by which Jesus rose from the dead accomplishes our great redemption. Our spiritual resurrection from death to new life takes place as we are united to him by the work of the Spirit (cf. Colossians 3:1–3). So Jesus' resurrection is not only proof of the completion and acceptance of his sacrifice for our sin, but it also shows his sovereign power to save and preserve. The Father gives this power to the Son, as proclaimed in Revelation 5:12: "Worthy is the Lamb that was slain to receive power and riches and wisdom and might and honor and glory and blessing" (cf. 1 Corinthians 1:24, Ephesians 1:19).

The surpassing greatness of his power toward us who believe is what has caused our rebirth to eternal life as God's children.

Knowing his saving mercy towards us is what gives the Christian 'a living hope' (1:3)—confidence and trust, knowing the certainty of God's faithfulness and power as our heavenly Father.

A lasting inheritance for you (1:4)

As scattered and persecuted Christians, the initial readers of Peter's epistle faced familial disinheritance and expulsion from the Jewish synagogue. Financial difficulty was also real, in a working world that expected engagement in pagan worship. In verse 4, Peter addresses this by pointing out another blessing of being rebirthed as a child of the Father. Not only is a new living hope now part of life—the Christian is also born again 'to an inheritance' (1:4).

Peter does not define the content of the inheritance here, though he gives some further reference to it in verse 5. In his second epistle Peter is more explicit, stating that, "according to his promise we are waiting for new heavens and a new earth in which righteousness dwells" (2 Peter 3:13). The Scriptures are clear: central to the believer's inheritance is God himself. "I am your share and inheritance" (Numbers 18:20). The book of Revelation displays this glorious reality perhaps most fully (cf. Revelation 21–22). The inheritance of Father's children is vast: new heavens and a new earth, the new Jerusalem, the heavenly city come to earth. But central to it all, just as with Aaron and the Levites, is the Lord himself. Perfect fellowship with the fullness of the Godhead revealed bodily, with God in Christ, is the believer's inheritance—dwelling in his presence, seeing him face to face, rejoicing in him, and he in us.

Peter does, however, describe the characteristics of this inheritance, with striking alliteration in the Greek.[3] It is 'imperishable' (1:4)—indestructible. Unlike the stuff of this world, your inheritance cannot go bad, cannot decay, or die. It is 'undefiled' (1:4), incorruptible. Your inheritance is not stained by any sin, and it is unable to be. It is perfect, good, and holy. It 'will not fade away' (1:4). Your inheritance will not slowly disappear over time, or get used up through eternity. It is reserved, 'kept in heaven' (1:4). The inheritance is ready and waiting. While we already experience glimmers and foretastes of it, when this earthly pilgrimage is completed, the Christian will receive the fullness of this inheritance made ready and kept by God, "let us rejoice and exult and give him glory, for the marriage of the Lamb has come ... Behold the dwelling place of God is with man" (Revelation 19:7, 21:3). All of this is kept by God 'for you' (1:4).

Guarded by God (1:5)

Peter's first readers may well have thought at this point, "This is all good and well, the inheritance is secured by God, it is secure, permanent and eternal, but what if I fail in the end to persevere? What if I am disqualified in the end? What if persecution should become so severe that I crack, I fail, I am unfaithful to Christ?"

God the Father is the one who has caused us to be born again by the Spirit, and Peter now reminds us that our spiritual protection and preservation as children is also the Father's work. He guards and sustains his children, faithful to complete the good work begun in them (cf. Philippians 1:6; Romans 8:31–39). God's power preserves us.

Peter instructs us further in verse 5, revealing one of the means by which God guards and preserves his people: 'who by God's power are being guarded through faith' (1:5). Faith is God's gift, the Spirit's work by the Word. It is the saving grace by which we receive and rest on Christ alone for our salvation. Faith consists of knowledge, conviction, and trust. By faith we are justified, by faith we are united to Christ, and it is God who preserves us in faith—and through faith—until this earthly race is complete, our salvation fully realized, and our faith made sight.

There is no greater power than God. He is omnipotent; all power is his. Peter reminds us in his second epistle that the power of God's word reserves the present heavens and earth for fire, for the day of judgment of ungodly men in which the heavens will pass away with a roar and the elements will be destroyed with intense heat (cf. 2 Peter 3:7–10). The God who spoke the universe into existence is the one preserving it for that day, just as by his power he is preserving his people for that day, 'for a salvation ready to be revealed in the last time' (1:5). This salvation includes the rich inheritance to which Peter just pointed us. It is a salvation so great that the apostle Paul exclaims, "no eye has seen, nor ear heard, nor the heart of man imagined, what God has prepared for those who love him" (1 Corinthians 2:9).

You and the Word

The Heidelberg Catechism (1563) beautifully echoes these verses of Peter's first epistle, answering the question, "What is your only comfort in life and in death?"

> That I am not my own, but belong—body and soul, in life and death—to my faithful Savior Jesus Christ. He has fully paid for all my sins with his precious blood, and has set me free from the tyranny of the devil. He also watches over me in such a way that not a hair can fall from my head without the will of my Father in heaven: in fact, all things must work together for my salvation. Because I belong to him, Christ, by his Holy Spirit, assures me of eternal life and makes me wholeheartedly willing and ready from now on to live for him.[4]

Are you rejoicing and resting in Christ's saving work? Are you trusting in the Redeemer sent in love so that you, a rebel sinner, could freely receive forgiveness from, reconciliation with, transformation in, and restoration to God? Are you filled with thankfulness as you consider your new life in Christ as a child of the Father, your secure and coming inheritance from him, and his powerful care for you? Join with Peter in blessing the God and Father of our Lord Jesus Christ!

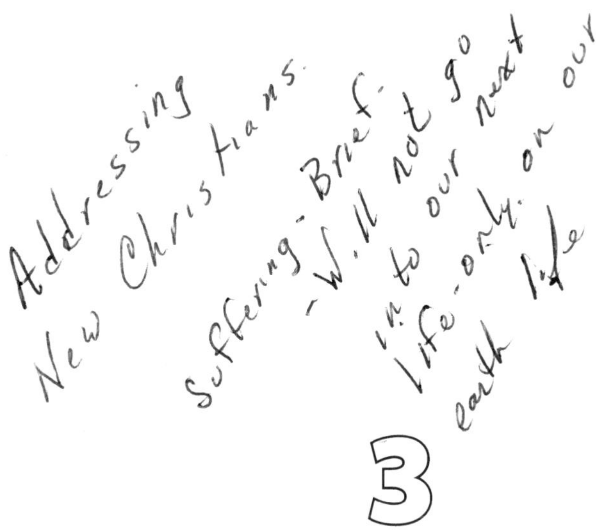

3

The Testing of Your Faith

Please read 1 Peter 1:6–9

Rejoicing while suffering (1:6)

Peter notes here that the church is rejoicing and will 'rejoice' (1:6) as it considers God's love and power displayed to them in their redemption (verses 2–3), their reserved inheritance (verse 4), and the protection of God that they enjoy (verse 5), as he keeps them for the great day of complete salvation. Much like the returning exiles of Nehemiah's day who "rejoiced, for God had made them rejoice with great joy" (Nehemiah 12:43), the New Testament church's reflection on what God has done, is now doing, and will do for them, fills them with great joy. Their joy is in the one who is so full of mercy, grace, and love towards them. Edmund Clowney says that Peter "is thinking, not just of all the blessings we have in Christ, but of Christ in whom we have the blessings."[1]

Part of the context of this exultant joy is present hardship. Real suffering occurs in the life of the church as Peter writes;

their rejoicing is juxtaposed with the fact that they are 'grieved by various trials' (1:6). Scripture does not minimize the legitimacy of sorrow or the reality of difficulty in the Christian's life. Instead, it calls God's people to place these things in the context of greater, enduring realities he has just described (verses 1–5). Peter wants us to join Paul in declaring, "I consider that the sufferings of this present time are not worthy to be compared with the glory to be revealed to us" (Romans 8:18). Above and beyond this he also provides a comforting, divine explanation of present suffering: these trials are 'for a little while,' and are only appointed by God 'if necessary' (1:6). While they are diverse and difficult, God specifically appoints and limits them in their nature, extent, and duration. What purpose could painful trials in life, even persecutions, serve for the child of God? Peter, by the Spirit, tells us they exist only when necessary for our good, and the glory of God.

Tested and proved (1:7)

Our faith goes through trials in the same way that gold is purified; impurities are burned out at high temperatures. But Peter notes the great difference—gold is perishable, our faith is not. No matter how hot the fire of the trial it cannot destroy our faith. We could think literally of the case of Shadrach, Meshach, and Abednego, or the torment of soul that the Psalmist endured—the fiery trials vary in their expression, but not in their cause and outcome. Trials will sanctify, strengthen, and display faith as an authentic, 'more precious than gold' (1:7) testimony to the sovereign grace of God. The 'tested genuineness of your faith' results 'in praise and glory and honor at the revelation of Jesus Christ' (1:7) (cf. 1 Thessalonians 1:10). By the Spirit, Peter closely echoes the language of Revelation with its declarations of praise to the Lamb who is worthy to receive honor and glory and blessing: "for you were slain, and by your blood you ransomed people for God from every tribe and language and people and nation, and you have made them a kingdom and priests to our God, and they shall reign on the earth" (Revelation 5:9–10, 12).

Not yet, but soon (1:8)

Peter now fully shifts our attention from our trials to Jesus Christ himself. The church lives in anticipation of the day of his appearing, 'the revelation of Jesus Christ' (1:7). She does so not by sight, but in faith. Verse 8 beautifully expresses love and great joy. The language evokes the picture of an exuberant bride longingly waiting for the arrival of her bridegroom. If you have been with a bride in the back of a church, you know the tense excitement that Peter implies here.

None of us have seen Jesus; neither had the believers to whom Peter wrote. 'Though you have not seen him, you love him. Though you do not now see him, you believe in him and rejoice with joy that is inexpressible and filled with glory' (1:8). As a disciple and apostle, though, he had seen Jesus. Here, as Christ's under-shepherd (John 21:15–17), Peter encourages us in the joy that our present faith will be made sight. If you are a Christian, you are going to see Jesus, the one who you love, the one whom you know in faith by Word, sacrament, and Spirit. The day is coming when he will be glorified in you, when you see him with your eyes, and you will marvel and be filled with joy, thrill, wonder, love and worship as you never have before. This is solid reason to run your race of life with endurance, "looking to Jesus, the founder and perfecter of our faith" (Hebrews 12:2).

Looking to the finish (1:9)

Peter's concluding clause reminds Christians of the consequence or 'outcome of your faith' (1:9). It is 'the salvation of your souls' (1:9). The language Peter uses brings out the sense of both individuality and plurality: the salvation of each believer and all the church will come to full completion at the revelation of Jesus Christ. Peter's use of the term "souls" does not negate the body, but is rather used holistically to refer to the entire existence or being of the believer, carrying with it the implication of the hope of the resurrection.[2]

You and the Word

John Brown of Edinburgh states that the trials of life that bring us "heaviness of heart" are "but for a season":

> [God] does not afflict willingly, nor grieve without a cause. Everything in the saint's lot is arranged in the way best suited to promote his true, his everlasting welfare. But in the future state there will be no heaviness, no, not even for a season ... Affliction will have served its purpose, and will forever cease. There, then, will be nothing but unmingled happiness and unending rejoicing ... The ransomed of the Lord shall return and come to Zion with songs, and with everlasting joy ... The Lamb who is in the midst of the throne shall feed them, and lead them to fountains of living waters; and God shall wipe away all tears from their eyes.[3]

The contrast with the unbeliever is stark: he lives in empty pursuits, without purpose in suffering. He is a rebel before God, heading for eternal judgment. But nothing is better, nothing gives sweeter hope and consolation now than life in communion with God in Christ. Even in grief, painful circumstances, and earthly uncertainty, the Christian can rest, knowing that God works all things together for good to those who love him (Romans 8:28). Live in light of the gracious, comforting truths spoken to you in these verses by the risen and ascended Savior.

> God moves in a mysterious way his wonders to perform;
> He plants his footsteps in the sea, and rides upon the storm.

Deep in unfathomable mines of never failing skill
He treasures up his bright designs, and works his sovereign will.

Ye fearful saints, fresh courage take; the clouds ye so much dread
Are big with mercy, and shall break in blessings on your head.[4]

Holy Anticipation

Please read 1 Peter 1:10–12

The prophets' great interest (1:10–11)

The 'salvation' (1:10) Peter speaks of here is that "salvation of your souls" (verse 9) which he described in the previous verses (cf. 1 Peter 1:5). It is the Triune God's salvation—planned by the Father, accomplished through the Son, and applied by the Holy Spirit. Peter's emphasis in these verses is on the eschatological fullness of this salvation. He wants us to keep in view the outcome and completion of our salvation at the second coming of our glorious King of kings and Lord of lords. The grandeur, glory and beauty of this salvation is immense. In verse 10, Peter highlights for us the prophets' desire to more fully understand this gracious work. These inspired men who 'prophesied about the grace that was to be yours' (1:10) studied it with devoted anticipation and wonder. They were eager to know as fully, precisely, and clearly as possible just how God would accomplish the redemption of his people.

As eager Old Testament students of the Word of God, the prophets wanted to know who the Messiah would be and when he would come. They wanted to know more fully the 'person' and 'time the Spirit of Christ in them was indicating' (1:11). The whole of Old Testament history and divine revelation drove forward to this culmination and fulfillment (cf. Genesis 3:15; Isaiah 9:6–7, 52:13–53:12). The prophets knew that a final, once-for-all sacrifice would be made (Hebrews 10:1–10). They knew that their sin needed blood atonement; they knew that God himself would provide. They knew that the Christ would be a suffering servant, one who would also bring God's people into new life, eternal fellowship with God, and great glory. Christ made this known to them, by his Spirit.

Having pastorally addressed the sufferings of the church and set them in the context of the glories to come (verses 3–9), Peter now uses the prophets to draw the reader's attention to 'the sufferings of Christ and the subsequent glories' (1:11) As God had promised, Jesus fulfilled all righteousness and bore the judicial penalty due to his people (Romans 5:6–21). He suffered, and the completion of his suffering is sealed in "the subsequent glories" of his resurrection, ascension, and session at the Father's right hand. The message to the church is twofold. First, the Triune God is ever faithful to his word; his promises are sure. Second, Christ the Eternal Son has opened the way to glory by his sufferings, we who live by faith in him through suffering will also enter into his glory (Isaiah 62).

The purpose of prophecy and preaching (1:12)

Peter continues to comfort the church by showing us the grand reality of which, as believers, we are part. By the Spirit he makes us aware that thousands of years ago, in the days of ancient civilizations, men of God were speaking about and looking forward to the day of salvation. In their ministries, the prophets were aware that 'they were not serving themselves but you' (1:12). Jude tells us that Enoch, "in the seventh generation from Adam, prophesied saying, "Behold the Lord comes with ten thousands of his holy ones" (Jude 14), Job declares, "I know that my Redeemer lives, and I will see Him in my flesh" (Job 19:23–27). Abraham prophetically promises that, "God will provide for himself the lamb for a burnt offering" (Genesis 22:8). Isaiah proclaims, "A Redeemer will come to Zion" (Isaiah 59:20) and "they will declare My glory among the nations" (Isaiah 66:19). Haggai communicates God's message that "in a little while ... I will shake all nations, so that the treasures of all nations shall come in, and I will fill this house with glory ... the latter glory of this house shall be greater than the former" (Haggai 2:6–9). There is, Peter reminds us, a "great cloud of witnesses" that surround us, having already run the race (Hebrews 12:1–2).

Not only did all of the prophets share in this eager anticipation for the unfolding and completion of God's mighty redemption, but also those 'who preached the good news to you' (1:12) in the present. The apostles, and the preachers who succeed them, are now able to announce by the Holy Spirit the fullness of Christ's first coming and his accomplished earthly ministry and substitutionary atonement. Yet anticipation remains. These ministers of the Word eagerly wait for and proclaim the approaching completion of Christ's work of redemption. They look forward with us to the day when the church is complete and "the Lord Jesus is revealed from heaven, with his mighty angels in flaming fire ... when he comes on that day to be glorified in his saints" (2 Thessalonians 1:7–9).

The interest in the great salvation of sinners is not limited to man. These are 'things into which angels long to look' (1:12). There is a cosmic interest in Christ's saving work. Redeemed men and holy angels, the "ministering spirits, sent out to serve for the sake of those who are to inherit salvation" (Hebrews

1:14), are gripped with interest in God's unfolding plan. The innumerable crowd of saints and angels serves Christ, working and watching for the coming marriage supper of the Lamb (Revelation 19:6–9). Earth itself has anticipation (Romans 8:19–22).

You and the Word

The tendency of the human heart is to focus on self and visible things. This remains a recurring problem for the Christian despite having come out of spiritual darkness and into God's marvelous light. In his *Religious Affections* Jonathan Edwards states that because of remaining sin our vision of God and his gracious work is too small and easily diminished: we have "distempers of the eyes" and "sight enfeebled."[1] Too often we are fearful and doubtful instead of joyful and certain. A lack of spiritual vision makes us prone to sin instead of passionate pursuit of thankful service to God. Peter, the apostle, delivers the Spirit's antidote. He places us in the company of saints, angels, and our Savior himself. Our understanding of history, our current situation and world, and the future, is realigned and our spiritual vision restored. As you study this portion of God's Word, make the words of this ancient Irish hymn your prayer:

Be thou my vision, O Lord of my heart,
Naught be all else to me, save that thou art,
Thou my best thought by day or by night,
Waking or sleeping, thy presence my light.

High King of heaven, my victory won,
May I reach heaven's joys, O Bright heaven's sun!
Heart of my own heart, whatever befall,
Still be my vision, O Ruler of all.[2]

5

Holy Action

Please read 1 Peter 1:13–16

Preparing for action (1:13)

What are the implications of the accomplishment and application of Christ's redemptive work for us? Peter essentially says, "now that you have heard all of this, now that you know that it is the Triune God at work in you to salvation, don't merely wonder at it in mental contemplation, but focus on the implication of these glorious realities and prepare for action!" The language Peter uses in verse 13, 'therefore, preparing your minds for action,' can be more literally translated, "gird up your minds." The metaphor reflects a change: a man in the Roman Empire wearing a long toga, sitting or walking slowly, is called to reach down and tie up his robes for action. Christ's call by his apostle to us echoes the Old Testament command to eat the Passover meal ready for action, "with your belt fastened, your sandals on your feet, and your staff in your hand" (Exodus 12:11). How do we gird up our minds for action?

The text tells us that being ready for action necessitates and includes 'being sober-minded' (1:13). We need to be clear headed, perceptive, and steady. Perhaps more than ever before in affluent, technologically advanced societies, there are countless things which can distract, mislead, or ensnare us, clouding and confusing our minds. Robert Leighton, reflecting on the call to sober-mindedness, notes that capitulating to the loves or lusts of this world, "injures the soul in its spiritual condition, makes it sickly and feeble, full of spiritual distempers and inactivity, benumbs the graces of the Spirit, and fills the soul with sleepy vapors, makes it grow heavy and secure in spiritual exercises, and obstructs the way and motion of the Spirit in the soul."[1] By contrast, an active and healthy prayer life, regular time in the Word, engagement in public worship, and Christian fellowship are all God-given means to grow in sober-mindedness.

The mental readiness and clarity that Peter calls us to has a focal point and goal: 'set your hope fully on the grace that will be brought you at the revelation of Jesus Christ' (1:13). Setting our hope and focus on God's grace and the consummation of our salvation reorients us God-ward. It assists in freeing us from "every weight, and sin which clings so closely" (Hebrews 12:1). This forward and upward hope in the all-sufficient grace of Christ, who "began the good work in you" and "will bring it to completion" (Philippians 1:6), lifts our spirits causing us to "mount up with wings like eagles" to "run and not be weary ... [and] walk and not faint." (Isaiah 40:31). Set in the context of the previous verses that anticipate Christ's work, heeding the call to be sober minded by setting our hope on Christ's second coming readies us to follow our Lord's commands. In the midst of the vast, glorious reality of God's sovereignty and Christ's person and work, we can run our earthly race through this fallen world with passion and focus.

Taking action: "Be holy, for I am holy" (1:14–16)

Parenting can be difficult. So when children are obedient, having fun, and experiencing joy in family life with their parents, it is not just wonderful for children, but also a delight to their parents. God desires the same for us in relationship to him. He is our heavenly Father. We owe him all we have and are; he created and redeemed us to find joy, fulfillment, and goodness as his 'obedient children' (1:14).

With this loving address comes a warning: 'do not to be conformed to the passions of your former ignorance' (1:14). We need to be wary of our own former sinful desires. The sins that used to entangled us can rise up again—along with new sins—within our hearts and minds. It is a present danger even for the strongest of Christians. Sin remains in us during this life, retaining a power to distort and damage. John Owen's sober statement that we must "be killing sin or it will be killing [us],"[2] sums up one aspect of the calling given to us here.

The other, positive aspect follows in the form of a similarly strong imperative: 'as he who called you is holy, you also be holy in all your conduct' (1:15). Rather than being conformed to sin, those whom God has called are "to be conformed to the image of his Son" (Romans 8:29). The flip side of the of putting sin to death cutting it off, is living in holiness. We cannot as Christians merely seek to negate sin, or we become like the parable of the house that was cleaned out and left empty. Jesus tells us that in the end it was worse than it at first, as wickedness quickly returned to fill the void (Matthew 12:43–45; Luke 11: 24–26). We are to be positively, not negatively or passively, holy in all our conduct, pursuing all the fruit of the Spirit, in communion with and conformity to our God.

Why are we to be holy? 'Since it is written, You shall be holy, for I am holy' (1:16). This quotation from Leviticus 11:44 stands in parallel with verse 15: twice here Peter tells us that God is holy. Between those statements of his holiness we are twice called to holiness in every aspect of our life and being. God is holy—the One before whom even the holy angels cover themselves as they cry, "Holy, holy, holy is the LORD of hosts; the whole earth is full of his glory!" (Isaiah 6:3). His will is that by his grace, we, strive with all our heart, soul, mind, and strength towards perfect, complete holiness in this life. His promise is not only that there is atonement for our sin in Christ, but also victory against sin in sanctification by his Spirit. At death, glorification will make the believer perfect and complete in holiness.

You and the Word

Where are you spiritually? Is your heart filled with wonder at the work Christ has accomplished for salvation? Is your heart filled with anticipation to see the continuation and completion of Jesus' work in you, the church, and creation? As you receive the riches and high calling of his Word, pray:

> Holy Triune God, thank you for your great work of redemption accomplished in Christ. Change me, help me prepare my mind for action, help me to be spiritually clear headed, sober-minded; take away the distractions, the fogs and dullness caused by my sin. Forgive and cleanse me from my many sins against you. Fix my hope completely on the great grace that will be brought to me at the glorious coming of your Son, on your return Lord Jesus, that I would live with anticipation the way the saints in heaven and angels do right now. Lord, help me to take action: to put sins to death, and with gratitude to work, exercise, battle for holiness in all of my life—that I would be living to your glory and praise more and more, that I would be an increasing blessing to your church, to family and friends. LORD bless and keep me, in Jesus name. Amen.

Holy Fear and Trusting Faith

Please read 1 Peter 1:17–21

Holy Fear, Knowing the Father (1:17)

Where in verse 16 Peter proclaimed the God-given call "you shall be holy, for I am holy," he now turns to a rhetorical question: do you address God as Father? Just as the believers to whom Peter wrote, we can also answer, yes, we do. We call God Father, often praying the Lord's prayer: "Our Father in heaven, hallowed be your name." (Matthew 6:9). Peter tells us that 'if you call on him as Father' (1:17), then there is a reality of which you need to be aware. The great, holy, triune God whom you address as Father, the one who rebirthed and adopted you, is the one 'who judges impartially according to each one's deeds' (1:17). The tense here is present—God is presently, actively judging every individual's deeds, now already. His knowledge of us is perfect; his evaluation and record of us is complete. "No creature is hidden from his sight, but all are naked and exposed to the eyes of him to whom we must give account" (Hebrews 4:13).

Knowing God's active judgment, you are to 'conduct yourselves with fear' (1:17). We are to live lives ordered in light of God's holy omniscience and perfect assessment of us towards his final judgment. Understanding this ultimate context of life before God should result in a reverential fear and carefulness, knowing, as Robert Leighton comments, "the highest anger and enmity of all the world [is] less than nothing, in comparison with his smallest displeasure."[1] Our Lord proclaimed, "Do not fear those who kill the body, and after that have nothing more that they can do. I will warn you who to fear: fear him who, after he has killed, has authority to cast into hell. Yes, I tell you, fear him!" (Luke 12:5).

Scripture indicates that when believers become cogently aware that they are in God's holy presence, their response is profound, reverential fear (Job 42:1–6, Isaiah 6:5, Revelation 1:17). In God's children, this fear is in harmony with trust, joy, and love towards him. Leighton points out that, "The more a Christian believes, and loves, and rejoices in the love of God, the more unwilling surely he is to displease him ... this fear being the true principle of a wary and holy [life], fleeing sin ... and temptations to it ... as a guard keeps out the enemies and disturbers of the soul."[2] Fear is not the same thing as being scared. Fear helps preserve the Christian's assurance of faith, confident hope, joy in God, and sweet fellowship with him. A spirit of reverential fear towards our heavenly Father is an essential ingredient of Christian life here and now—needed 'throughout the time of your exile' (1:17). Peter raises the theme of exile here for the second time (cf. verse 1) again reminding us that Christians are strangers and pilgrims in this world, desiring "a better country ... a heavenly one" (Hebrews 11:16).

Holy Fear, Knowing the Cost of Redemption (1:18–19)

The apostle of our Lord continues in verse 18 by telling us that we are to conduct ourselves with fear, 'knowing that you were ransomed from the futile ways inherited from your forefathers' (1:18). Our inherited pursuit of life in sin is a futile pursuit of self-destruction, damage to others, and disobedience towards God, leading to certain judgment. Worshipping the creature rather than the Creator (Romans 1:25) accomplishes nothing of enduring value, brings no lasting satisfaction or joy, and leaves us exposed to God's righteous, eternal wrath. The fact that by our old nature and desire we were in headlong pursuit of such futility, warns and reminds us that since we have been enlightened (Hebrews 6:4) and richly blessed with new life, we are to conduct ourselves in thankful reverence and holiness to God.

This is all the more the case when we consider the great cost of our redemption from sin: 'you were ransomed … not with perishable things such as silver or gold, but with the precious blood of Christ, like that of a lamb without blemish or spot' (1:19). The redemption of sinners and their restoration to God is extremely expensive. Its cost is far beyond the most precious, temporary stuff of this earth. It is beyond the ability of men or angels to bridge the infinite divide between a sinner and the holy God. It could only be accomplished by one of infinite worth, by one who is always worthy. The great mystery of God's love and grace is that he would and did freely act in, through, and upon his only begotten Son. Jesus is the only one who could make the payment for the salvation of men. Commenting on Christ's substitutionary sacrifice, John Murray states

> the work of Christ is expiatory, expiatory with transcendent virtue, efficacy, and perfection that could not apply to bulls and goats, yet expiatory in terms of the pattern provided by the Old Testament sacrificial ritual. This means that to him, as the great

> sacrifice offered without spot to God, were transferred the sins and liabilities of those on whose behalf he offered himself a sacrifice. By reason of this imputation he suffered and died, just for unjust, that he might bring us nigh to God. By one sacrifice he hath perfected forever all them that are sanctified.[3]

The message of Christ's great atoning work (1:18) echoes Hebrews, which tells us that Christ, "entered once for all into the holy place, not by means of the blood of goats and calves but by means of his own blood, thus securing an eternal redemption" (Hebrews 9:12). Knowing that the cost for the atonement of your sin against God is the blood of Christ, the eternal Son of God, gives vast reason and motive to conduct yourself in reverential fear.

Trusting Faith, Knowing God's Love in Christ (1:20–21)

Our awareness of the grandeur and wonder of salvation, of the eternal purposes carried out in time by God to redeem a people to himself, is further increased in verse 20. Here Peter states that '[Christ] was foreknown before the foundation of the world but was made manifest in the last times' (1:20). Peter echoes the opening verses of the epistle, pointing the reader to God's sovereign purpose for salvation. The Triune God planned and purposed Christ's saving work from eternity and fulfilled it in time. This is how Old Testament believers were saved—Christ's work already had efficacious, retrospective value for them as they, by faith in God's covenant promise, made temple sacrifices that point to Christ's coming atonement. Now, Jesus has come in time, been revealed, and has accomplished it. Both his costly work of atonement and his self-revelation as the Savior are 'for the sake of you, who through him are believers in God' (1:21). This is why he shed his blood and revealed himself by his Word.

And God has accepted his work. It was confirmed in his resurrection, ascension, and glorification: 'God ... raised him from the dead and gave him glory' (1:21). Why? 'So that your faith and hope are in God' (1:21). The glorious realities of God's saving work in Christ have direct, personal connection to the believer. God has accomplished and applied it all specifically for your sake, so that you would live by faith and hope in God.

You and the Word

As you read these verses meditate on their incredible richness as the Word of God to you. God desires that you be filled with a holy, reverential fear and trusting faith towards him as your Father. The Word calls us to live our lives with an intentional, diligent care in the pursuit of holiness. God has provided an answer for our sin, our disobedience, our violation of his holiness, and our need for new life, a right spirit, and strength to pursue holiness—all in Jesus Christ.

In Christ, God has accomplished everything needed for your salvation. Christ is now seated on the throne of glory as the first-fruits, the God man, the Eternal Son made flesh, the Savior. He is the one who made the once for all, costly sacrifice, satisfying God's just penalty for his people's sins. We could not do this for ourselves even by eternity in hell. Jesus serves as the eternal high priest—the mediator between holy God and sinful men, for us (Hebrews 4:14–16). He is risen from the dead, ascended and reigning in glory, so that you can live by faith with confidence in God.

Were the whole realm of nature mine,
That were a present far too small;
Love so amazing, so divine,
Demands my soul, my life, my all.[4]

7

The Eternal Word and Christian Love

Please read 1 Peter 1:22–2:3

Brotherly Love (1:22–23)

The action of planting seeds enables new life to begin, then bear fruit. Verses 22 of chapter one through verse 3 of chapter two contain a marvelous pattern. The text flows from the new life (1:22), to the new birth (1:23) and then the Word (1:23–25), and then back again to the call to live the new life, (2:1), like newborn infants drinking in the Word in order to grow (2:2–3).

Having just described God's work in Christ for your sake (1:20), Peter first draws our attention in verse 22 to a new characteristic which is to flourish in believers: love. Love is the fruit of saving faith in Jesus. Peter describes it as being consequent of 'having purified your souls by obedience to the truth' (1:22). God, who is love, sent his Son with the purpose of saving us from our own sin and enmity towards him, so that we would love him above all, and our neighbor as ourselves. He has saved us 'for a sincere brotherly love' (1:22), calling us to 'love one another earnestly from a pure heart' (1:22).

Just as in the first century church in Asia Minor, there are some people whom we find easy to love. Others are more difficult. Their personalities, quirks, or interests leave us disinterested, even irritated. Too often we comfortably assume we are fulfilling life in Christ in the church simply through outward cordiality; at times we feel like it is the maximum we can do. God, however, calls and enables us to something profoundly greater: his love. Like the Grinch's heart in the Christmas tale, our sin-shrunken hearts cannot naturally give it. This love is both different and greater. Merely knowing we need to love others does not create this love. The answer is not found within. Our Lord's loving joy is to recreate us, his church, to know, delight in, and share in Triune love. United to him, by the power of His Spirit, we are enabled to love each other (John 15:9–11). This love is without hypocrisy; it especially delights in and pursues all that is good for our brothers and sisters in Christ. This of course does not mean that the pursuit of earnest, Word shaped love will not bring suffering—it often does. The Father, Son, and Holy Spirit know this far more extensively than we will ever experience, and have on our behalf of us. But just as Christ's suffering for us did not diminish his earnest love for us, but displays it all the more vividly, neither should our love diminish because of suffering.

The Eternal Word (1:23–25)

The apostle connects the call to fervently love one another from the heart to God's regeneration of us. The reason that we have come to obey the gospel call to faith and repentance in Christ is because of the gracious work of the Holy Spirit; 'since you have been born again' (1:23). The new life planted in us brings new obedience and new love. The epistle almost becomes poetic here as Peter describes the reality of the new life begotten through the Word using the picture of seed, grass, and its flowers. We are naturally born 'of perishable seed' (1:23): our natural life with all its glories, is short-lived, quickly fading away. 'All flesh is like grass, and all its glory like the flower of the grass. The grass withers, and the flower falls' (1:24). These words are poignant and sober. We, like the grass, only remain for a short season before we wither away to death. "Time, like an ever rolling stream, bears all its sons away." If this is the sum total of reality we can well conclude "vanity of vanities, all is vanity" (Ecclesiastes 1:2).

Looking to the text, we see two contrasts, marked with the word "but". Verse 23 tells us that we have been born again, 'not of perishable seed but of imperishable' (1:23). There is a glorious God-given answer to the inevitable decay to death of a rebel humanity under the curse. It begins with the seed of 'the living and abiding Word of God' (1:23): as it is read and preached, its imperishable seed is planted in hearts and minds, germinating by the power of the Spirit within the human soul. There is a new creation and new life begun—and it can never decay. It can never die, because it is the work of the living God, who is always faithful: 'the Word of the Lord remains forever' (1:25). Peter reminds us that this unfailing 'word is the good news that was preached to you' (1:25). The whole of God's Word, from Genesis 1:1 through Revelation 22:21 is good news: it proclaims to us God's salvation in Christ. God intends that his Word bring us into eternal life with him. He has spoken this Word to us. He desires that we have full confidence in him and in what he has said to us.

Cultivating Growth in Grace (2:1–3)

Having called us to love one another earnestly from a pure heart through the imperishable source of new life in God, Peter now turns to a corresponding imperative: 'put away all malice and all deceit and hypocrisy and envy and all slander' (2:1). While we all have some understanding of these sins, being reminded of what they are is essential to discerning and killing their presence within us. Malice is "the intention or desire to do evil." It is ill will to others. Deceit is "the action or practice of deceiving someone by concealing or misrepresenting the truth." Hypocrisy is saying we have moral or ethical standards that we do not live by. Envy is "a feeling of discontented or resentful longing aroused by someone else's possessions, qualities, or situation." Slander is "making a false spoken statement damaging to a person's reputation."[1]

These are the ugly opposite of genuine love. Love builds up, these destroy. Apart from Christ, sin dominates in its strength. In Christ we not only receive forgiveness, but by his Spirit we also receive grace and power to gain victory over sin, replacing it with the new life of love.

While spiritual maturity over time is real, none of us have "arrived," either in extinguishing these sins from our lives or in being fully loving. Peter uses a humbling analogy to direct us to the means of personal and relational spiritual growth: 'like newborn infants, long for the pure spiritual milk, that by it you may grow up into salvation—if indeed you have tasted that the Lord is good' (2:2–3). In Peter's day, merchants would often water down milk or wine, but the word Peter uses describes milk that is whole and pure. We need to regularly and eagerly drink in the Word to experience healthy Christian growth. If you have tasted the Lord's goodness you will want to!

You and the Word

Reflecting on this passage, John Brown of Edinburgh wrote:

> Like newborn infants, the Christian has a kind of instinctive, unquenchable desire after the suitable spiritual [nourishment] of

> his new nature. He loves the truth as it is in Jesus; he is restless when it is out of view ... The whole world without this cannot make him happy; and he never enjoys himself more, than when clearly apprehending the meaning ... of those "exceedingly great and precious promises" by which his new nature is sustained.[2]

God has encouraged and challenged you in these verses to the active pursuit of growth in new life, by his grace and faithfulness. With gladness for God's undeserved, complete love to you, prayerfully pursue an intentional plan for greater saturation in his Word, and a greater love for the fellow believers that make up your church community. Search your heart and your relationships, to see where your sin continues to hinder and mar the life of the body; confess all to the Lord, receiving his forgiveness and strength to put evil to death, and to grow in all that is good and holy.

> Christ of all my hopes the ground ...
> Let your love my heart inflame;
> Keep your fear before my sight;
> Be your praise my highest aim;
> Be your smile my chief delight.[3]

Like Living Stones

Please read 1 Peter 2:4–8

Coming to the Living Stone (2:4)

To us, as to the first readers of the epistle, the language of a living stone is a paradox; it sounds unlike anything we've seen. Where has Peter drawn this from? Why is he referring to our Lord Jesus Christ as 'a living stone' (2:4)?

For Jewish and Gentile believers who had at one point in their lives had gone up to Jerusalem to worship, this language called to mind the earthly center of Old Testament worship at the temple: a tangible picture of grandeur, beauty, solidity and strength. The word "stone" Peter uses describes a stone used in construction. The wider context makes it clear that he is alluding to the massive marble blocks used in the temple, some weighing twenty tons. In the gospels, Peter was impressed by these stones, saying to Jesus, "Look, Teacher, what wonderful stones and what wonderful buildings!" (Mark 13:1–2). And yet, as the Old Testament taught, and as Jesus plainly declared, for all its splendor, the temple was an image, a type of a far greater reality. Hebrews tells us these were copies of the heavenly realities (Hebrews 9:23–24, 10:19–22), pictures of Christ's person and work in restoring us to life with God. This is why Jesus told Peter and the rest of the disciples not to put their hope in the magnificence of the earthly temple (Mark 13:2), but in himself, the one who is "greater than the temple" (Matthew 12:16).

Not only is Peter aware of Jesus' teaching about the temple and himself; he also draws directly on the fulfillment of Old Testament prophecy in referring to Jesus as the living stone. Isaiah declared that the LORD was laying "a foundation in Zion, a stone, a tested stone, a precious cornerstone," fulfilling his covenant promise to everyone who believes (Isaiah 28:16–18). The reality that Peter shares is that Christ is this stone. He is the foundation for the whole church and he lives. Matthew Henry says:

> In this metaphorical description of Jesus Christ, he is called a stone, to denote his invincible strength and everlasting duration, and to teach his servants that he is their protection and security, the foundation on which they are built ... He is the living stone, having eternal life in Himself, and being the prince of life to all his people.[1]

Jesus Christ's invincible strength as the living stone is displayed in the fact that he is risen from the dead. Despite the fact that he was, and is, 'rejected by men, in the sight of God' he is 'chosen and precious' (2:4). Our strong and sure Redeemer King is the joy of the Father—all the more reason for our complete confidence in God.

Being built up as a spiritual house (2:5)

As we come to Jesus, the living stone, an amazing reality takes place: 'you yourselves like living stones, we are built up as a spiritual house' (2:5). This is astounding. The picture is of a temple-building construction scene: you and I are part of God's continually growing temple. We, who are sinners, are united to Christ the living stone, made living stones in union with him, built up in communion with him for service to him. Not only is God building the church as his dwelling place, as every believer is individually, but through the new birth we are also inaugurated 'to be a holy priesthood, to offer spiritual sacrifices acceptable to God through Jesus Christ' (2:5). This was the purpose God gave to Adam and Eve in the Garden: to glorify God and enjoy him forever. This is the purpose for our regeneration, renewal, and reconciliation to God (cf. Romans 12:1–2). This is what we now are in Christ: holy priests, enabled through him to offer up sacrifices of praise and service acceptable to God.

Christ, the cornerstone (2:6–8)

Not long ago, Peter reminded us of our need to be saturated in the "word of the Lord [which] remains forever" (1:25). While Peter continues to pen that very Word, he echoes the principle that, "man shall not live by bread alone, but by every word that comes from the mouth of God" (Deuteronomy 8:3; Matthew 4:4). Highlighting the centrality of Jesus Christ in our salvation and service to God, Peter cites Isaiah: 'Behold, I am laying in Zion a stone, a cornerstone chosen and precious, and whoever believes in him will not be put to shame' (2:6; cf. Romans 9, 10).[2] God's Word is faithful and true, his promises are always fulfilled. We have no reason to doubt that we are welcomed to come to Christ and be secure in him. While we may be the despised of the world, we need not fear shame. Not only do we have every reason for confidence, but in Christ we are also brought into a relationship and place of honor—'the honor is for you who believe' (2:7). We are now God's sons, and as sons, heirs with

Christ, welcomed into the love of the Triune God. There is no better place to be.

On the contrary, 'for those who do not believe, "The stone that the builders rejected has become the cornerstone," and "A stone of stumbling, and a rock of offense"' (2:7–8). Rejecting Christ does nothing to thwart his mission or glory, as his earthly ministry made clear. No one can stop the Trinity's redemptive plan. Those who do not believe, stumble over Christ. His person and work offends them. They reject the gospel because Jesus is an offense to their pursuit of sin. They are offended by his holiness. They are offended because they do not want to be humbled before God. They are offended because they think they are good enough in themselves and really do not need God's cornerstone. They think that they can build their own way to happiness, their own way to life, just as the builders of the Tower of Babel did. In response to the anger of the scribes and Pharisees at the parable of the owner of the vineyard, Jesus said to them, "What then is this that is written: 'The stone that the builders rejected has become the cornerstone? Everyone who falls on that stone will be broken to pieces, and when it falls on anyone, it will crush him'" (Luke 20:17–18). The unbeliever's rebellion against Christ is a rebellion of futility.

Peter concludes with the sober note of the full personal responsibility of the unbeliever in stumbling over and being offended by Christ: it is 'because they disobey the word' (2:8). Unbelief is not a result of a lack of Scripture's clarity or believability—it is simple disobedience. What can be known about God is plain to all of humanity in creation (Romans 1:19) and is just as plain in his Word. Yet even as a willful rebel, the unbeliever cannot escape God's sovereign rule: they disobey the word 'as they were destined to do' (2:8). They will continue in sin and rebellion because God, while revealing himself to them constantly, allows them to do what they want.

You and the Word

God's love to us in Christ is vast. God's mercy to us is that he has called us, brought us out of doing what we want in sinful rebellion, and given us new life in Christ. He has so loved the world that he gave his only begotten Son, that whoever believes in him should not perish but have eternal life (John 3:16). His Son is the living stone, the precious cornerstone of his salvation plan for us—a plan which goes far beyond the new birth to a new community of life in union with Christ and communion with God. God's people, his church, are his temple, the place where he delights to dwell and continue his gracious work. As you think over this passage, consider how you can grow in serving him as a member of his holy priesthood. What kinds of spiritual sacrifices can you offer up to God, through Christ? How can you grow in the quality of your reading and hearing his Word, praying, and singing to him? In what ways can you grow in serving him in his church?

Fill thou my life, O Lord my God,
In ev'ry part with praise,
That my whole being may proclaim
thy being and thy ways.

Not for the lip of praise alone,
Nor e'en the praising heart,
I ask, but for a life
Made up of praise in every part.[3]

Proclaiming the Excellencies of God

Please read 1 Peter 2:9–10

Understanding our new status (2:9)

Our passage begins with a "but." This little word signals an important transition. The previous verses concluded by unmasking the ugly reality of unbelief: those who stumble at Christ do so because they prefer to disobey. 'But' (2:9), Peter says to the church, though that is where you once were, you are not anymore! The situation for believers is radically different from those who remain God's enemies: 'you are a chosen race, a royal priesthood, a holy nation, a people for his own possession' (2:9).

What does it mean that 'you are a chosen race' (2:9)? Peter is drawing on the words of Exodus 19:5–6, but in a postmodern mindset this language can conjure up ideas of racial supremacism, with the term "chosen" indicating superiority. But that would be twisting the verse with our own cultural sins. Commentator Edmund Clowney begins to frame our thinking correctly here as he notes that Peter says chosen, not choice.[1] There is no room for pride or boasting here. As Christians, we were not chosen because of our ethnicity, intelligence, morality, or financial situation. It was not because there was something choice in us, or good or slightly better than in any other sin-loving, God-hating rebel (cf. Romans 3:9–19). In his first letter to the Corinthians, the apostle Paul says,

> consider your calling, brothers: not many of you were wise according to worldly standards, not many were powerful, not many were of noble birth. But God choose what was foolish in the world to shame the wise; God choose what is weak in the world to shame the strong ... so that no human being might boast in the presence of God. He is the source of your life in Christ Jesus ... Therefore it is written, "Let the one who boasts, boast in the Lord." (1 Corinthians 1:26–31)

Similarly, in Deuteronomy Israel is told "it was not because you were more in number than any other people that the Lord set his love on you and chose you, for you were the fewest of all peoples, but it is because the Lord loves you" (Deuteronomy 7:7–8). In love God chose to reconcile and restore us to himself, not merely as solitary individuals, but as a "race"—a family or people belonging to him. We are not only related in Adam, but in Christ we are also brought into a family relationship as children of God: a reality which transcends our natural families, interests and affiliations.

Peter further tells us that in Christ we are made a 'royal priesthood' (2:9). The true nobility, the true royalty of the earth is not the British monarchy, Hollywood stars, Chinese corporate executives, oil sheikhs, or the dictators of the world. While God has providentially ordained rulers and the influential of this earth, the true, enduring royalty are the people of King Jesus because we are united to Christ and joint-heirs with him. You are seated with Christ in the heavenly places (Ephesians 2:6). Christians, now already, share in Christ's reign, and will more fully to come (2 Timothy 2:12). Peter connects royal title with the priesthood of all believers. We are royal priests, offering up living sacrifices to God, made acceptable to God in Christ Jesus (Romans 12:1–2).

The church, as the body of Christ, is also 'a holy nation' (2:9). In the Old Testament context, particularly after the patriarchal period, Israel was the holy nation, with a few Gentiles grafted in. The New Testament context displays more fully the extent of God's saving plan, incorporating people of every nation, tribe, people, and language (Revelation 7:9). The church is a nation on a massive scale: globally extensive, and even cosmically extensive, as it extends to heaven itself and transcends time. This nation is as unique as it is holy, set apart to God and his glory, to dwell in holiness, righteousness, and peace forever through its mediatorial King. Being set apart to God, we are his in a special way: 'you are a people for his own possession' (2:9). We belong to God. These were incredibly precious words for the oppressed and despised Christians of Asia Minor; they are for us as well. No one loves us more, or blesses us more, than our God and Savior does. Though we are citizens of earthly countries with national passports, our enduring citizenship is in Heaven.

Proclaiming God's excellence (2:9–10)

Why has God lavished such love and kindness on us? So 'that you may proclaim the excellencies of him who called you out of darkness into his marvelous light' (2:9). Our God is excellent in who he is and what he has done, is doing, and will do for us. He created and recreated us to worship him (Isaiah 43:21). Just as the Israelites were delivered from the Angel of Death on the Passover night, a judgement that brought them deliverance from Egypt's oppression, so through the gospel call of the Lamb, he brings us out of our spiritual darkness into Christ's marvelous light (Psalm 36:9; John 1:1–16; 8:12). The word "proclaim" (2:9) calls for a passionate, clear declaration of praise—the only fitting response to our gracious God. To put it in a musical analogy, it is not a feeble, uncertain note, but a clear blast on a trumpet. Our praise-filled proclamation is centered on God: "to commemorate the saving deeds of the Lord is a thrilling task, but the pinnacle of devotion is to rejoice in God himself, the doer of these deeds."[2]

In verse 10 Peter gives us two parallel sets of contrasts as further motives to proclaim the excellencies of God. The first is a citation from Hosea, a book that proclaims God's unilateral saving love for a people who cared nothing for him: 'once you were not a people, but now you are the people of God' (2:10). The Lord reminds us here that it is good to remember what we were and would be, apart from him. We all need to do this, perhaps especially those nurtured in the faith in Christian families. We may not be able to remember a time when we were not Christians, but remembering God's gracious work in our lives is essential to guard us from the arrogant delusion that we were somehow "choice" in ourselves. An honest view of our sin will make us deeply grateful to God for his grace to us in Christ. It will fill us with amazement that we are now God's people!

The second contrast and motive to praise that Peter gives parallels the first: 'once you had not received mercy, but now you have received mercy' (2:10). Mercy is kindness to a person, especially to an enemy within our power. We are all within God's power; in sin we are all his enemies. Where we were once living in the lie and misery of sin, justly under his curse and facing his punishment (Psalm 5:5–6; John 3:36), through his mercy we will not receive from him what we deserve. Instead, we receive his kindness and forgiveness through Christ. Jesus has taken the penalty, the wrath that we deserve (Isaiah 53). We have received mercy from God!

You and the Word

These verses are packed with the goodness and grace of God to us, reminding us of who he is, causing our hearts to overflow with gratitude, love, and praise to him. Centuries before the coming of Christ, the prophet Isaiah, anticipating the grace of God through the Son, proclaimed:

> You will say in that day:
>
> "I will give thanks to you, O LORD, for though you were angry with me, your anger turned away that you might comfort me. Behold, God is my salvation; I will trust, and will not be afraid; for the LORD God is my strength and song, and he has become my salvation. With joy you will draw water from the wells of salvation."
>
> And you will say in that day:
>
> "Give thanks to the LORD, call upon his name, make known his deeds among the peoples, proclaim that his name is exalted. Sing praises to the LORD, for he has done gloriously; let this be made known in all the earth. Shout and sing for joy, O inhabitant of Zion, for great in your midst is the Holy One of Israel." (Isaiah 12:1–6)

Trust him and rejoice, for he is your salvation and your God.

10

Abstaining and Excelling

Please read 1 Peter 2:11–12

Who you are (2:11)

In light of all that our Lord has conveyed through Peter to the church, it is only fitting that the opening address in this verse is an expression of love. The church is the 'beloved' (2:11), not only of Peter, but beloved of God. The Scriptures often express this language as God speaks of his love for his people. In Exodus he declares, "I am the LORD your God," using language of love, of belonging. The Chronicler and Psalmists remind us that his steadfast love endures forever (2 Chronicles 5:13; Psalm 100:5). The love song of Solomon and his bride beautifully pictures and points forward to the fullness of Christ's love for the Church (Song of Solomon 2:16). When we come to the New Testament, the Father repeatedly reaffirms to Jesus, "You are my beloved Son, with you I am well pleased." (Mark 1:11; 2 Peter 1:17). God has so loved his church that he has sent this beloved Son for her redemption and restoration into the fellowship of his Triune love.

The fact that God's love has restored us to him means that we no longer are one with a world at enmity with God. We are 'sojourners and exiles' (2:11) here, "desiring a better country" (Hebrews 11:16). The more we walk in communion with and praise to God, the more we will appear to be strangers in communities still at odds with him. As Peter writes later in the epistle, "they are surprised when you do not join them in the same flood of debauchery, and they malign you" (1 Peter 4:4).

Abstaining from lusts (2:11)

Prefaced by this affirmation of love, Peter calls us to action: 'I urge you as sojourners and exiles to abstain from the passions of the flesh, which wage war against your soul' (2:11). Peter's call here is specifically to avoid things that promote the rise of sinful desires. Why? Because sinful passions and desires are deceitful and diametrically opposed to life with God in Christ; they are God's enemies, opposed to all that is good and holy. Like Satan, they aim to cripple you to the greatest extent possible.

While Jesus has broken sin's powerful rule for the Christian and enabled us to not sin, we are not yet free from sin. It remains an enemy lurking within. John Bunyan, a 17th century handyman, soldier, and preacher, wrote, *The Holy War—the Losing and Taking Again of the Town of Mansoul*. It is the story of a walled city once under the rule of Diabolus (Satan), but won over to El Shaddai.[1] In his captivating tale, Bunyan illustrates how sin rises again in our motives and desires, seeking to re-capture and re-dominate our whole being. God's Word gives us the awareness of this reality, the call to fight the good fight of hating and forsaking sin and the means to do so. We can pursue abstaining from the passions of the flesh by being scripturally self-aware, intentionally avoiding activities and contexts that would nurture sin, rather than holiness, in our lives (cf. Psalm 101:3; Hebrews 12:12–13).

Excelling in good deeds (2:12)

The pursuit of sanctification has two aspects: rooting out sin and cultivating the fruit of the Spirit. Ephesians calls it, "putting off" and "putting on" (Ephesians 4:22–24). Luke records that Jesus taught a parable of a man who had an evil spirit leave him and subsequently worked hard to clean out all the bad stuff in his life, only to find the evil spirit return with seven more, and to be worse off in the end (Luke 11:24–26). A healthy Christian life will not flourish if we only pursue abstaining from the passions of the flesh. We also need to pursue filling our hearts and lives with what is excellent and holy.

Verse 12 tells us 'keep your conduct among the Gentiles honourable so that when they speak against you as evildoers, they may see your good deeds and glorify God on the day of visitation' (2:12). Our lives are situated within surrounding communities, which in many cases are predominantly non-Christian. As we engage in work, commerce, and relaxation, we are to be characterized by honorable (also translated as excellent, beautiful, or honest) conduct. Why? So that a community still at enmity with God, still in the darkness of sin while repelled by the light, will still see the beauty of holiness. They will see and know that we are in fact people who do what is good; people who by God's grace are growing in goodness.

In relation to the final phrase of this verse—'and glorify God on the day of visitation' (2:12)—interpreters argue that perhaps two things are in view here. The first is that Peter may be anticipating a time when non-Christians who have mocked Christians for their faithful lives, are themselves transformed by Word and Spirit (cf. Luke 10:9–10). Many people have been drawn to Christ through the excellence of Christian conduct

(Matthew 5:16). They see and hear love, truth, purity, goodness and joy, the fruits of the Spirit, and are brought to repentance and faith through the powerful attraction of the loveliness of Christ, made evident in his restored people. God-haters become God-glorifiers.

The second reality in view is the day of God's visitation in judgment (Isaiah 10:3). At the great coming of "the day of the Lord" (2 Peter 3:10, 12), God's Son and his people will be vindicated. Every knee will bow, and every tongue confess that Jesus Christ is Lord (Romans 14:11; Philippians 4:10). Those who unrepentantly mocked God and slandered his gracious work in them will glorify God for who he is and what he has done. Both of these realities, God's visitation in grace and judgement, serve as a powerful impetus for us to live to his glory in the midst of a watching and listening world.

You and the Word

What practical, intentional steps can you take to both abstain from sinful passions and pursue excellent behavior in your life and relationships?

First, be sure that you are pursuing a close walk with God, communing with him in and through Christ. Ask him to "search me, O God, and know my heart! Try me and know my thoughts! And see if there be any grievous way in me, and lead me in the way everlasting" (Psalm 139:23–24). Come to him to receive the cleansing, forgiveness, grace, and wisdom you need for an increasingly faithful walk with him. Delight in prayer, the Word, and worship with his people.

Second, as you prayerfully consider areas of life where you know you have old or recurring dispositions to sin, pursue adjusting your life activities in ways that will cut off situations where you know you will be prone to temptation. This may mean changes in your evening entertainment choices, it may mean changes in your social life, or in your family habits—where previous patterns have fostered tendencies to sin, rather than growth in godliness.

Third, prayerfully consider how you can intentionally grow in God-honoring life in relation to those around you. How can you positively replace what has been negative? How can you more fully love God above all and your neighbor as yourself? How can you grow in bringing the truth and wisdom of God's Word into your conversations and actions? Consider this as you plan your week, as you plan each day. Make your plans in communion with Christ, your Savior and King. Ask God, by his Spirit, to give you what you need as his beloved to live more excellently in this present age.

What shall I render to my God for all his kindness shown?
My feet shall visit thine abode, my songs address thy throne.

How happy all thy servants are! How great thy grace to me!
My life, which thou hast made thy care, Lord, I devote to thee.[2]

Rome - Nero - Deeply corrupt -
mistrust of Christians

11

Christian Submission and Civil Government

Please read 1 Peter 2:13–17

Submitting to governing authorities (2:13–14)

When discussing a passage on obedience to governing authority it is easy for us to get off track. Some people launch into discussions of when and when not to obey civil authorities, ending up in debates over historical events ranging from the Zealots under Roman rule, to the American Revolution, or resistance movements under the Nazi regime. Others feel that this is an incidental area of life and want to move on to other things. But because Scripture is God's Word, everything in it is of significance for us. God's Word does not come to us to stir up philosophical or theoretical debates, but to transform our hearts, minds, and lives.

Consider the context of what Peter is about to tell us here. He has just shown us the rich blessings of salvation by Jesus' precious blood and the great change God has made in the lives of his people, to proclaim his excellencies and excel in holy living. In this context, Peter says, 'submit yourselves for the Lord's sake to every human institution, whether it be to the emperor as supreme, or to governors as sent by him to punish those who do evil and to praise those who do good' (2:13–14).

What is it to submit? Submitting is yielding to authority, giving obedience to a person or institution that God has placed in authority over us. The way Scripture uses this word in other places helps us get a better sense of what it means here. Peter uses it when he says, "likewise you younger, be subject to the elders" (1 Peter 5:5). The apostle James says, "submit yourselves therefore to God" (James 4:7). Our ultimate submission is to God.

Peter's focus in these verses is the specific call for our submission to governing authorities in the civil realm as followers of the Lord Jesus Christ. He mentions 'every human institution, the emperor' and regional 'governors' (2:14). Roman rule was often dictatorial and corrupt. It included a vast bureaucracy, with departments and laws regulating many aspects of life. For most of the Mediterranean world, Roman rule was a foreign imposition, made by military or political conquest. Taxes could be tremendously heavy, and were used to build not only roads and libraries, but also temples, theatres, and to support occupying military forces. While Roman government could oppress whole populations, it was often the main source of persecution of the Christian church. If our Lord called the Christians of Asia Minor to submit to human institutions of governance, how much more shouldn't we respectfully submit to our governments in the way the Word calls us to?

Why submit to our governments? (2:13–14)

Peter understood the challenges to the human heart in

submitting to any government and had undoubtedly heard the question, "but why submit to a government like this?" (John 18:10–11). The answer is simple: 'for the Lord's sake' (1:13). We do so for the sake of his commandment (cf. Matthew 22:21; Titus 3:1–2; Romans 13:1–7). We do so because he purchased us (1 Peter 1:3–4, 18–19; 2:9–10). We do so as we follow Jesus' own example to us (John 18:10–11; 19–24; 28–40). We do so for the sake of the expansion of his kingdom. Part of the gospel witness we present to the world is found in honoring those in authority over us, submitting to their rule respectfully wherever that does not come in conflict with God's law (Acts 5:29). By submitting to the rulers God has ordained, we adorn the gospel of the Lord Jesus Christ with good works, to his glory (1 Peter 2:12).

Peter encourages us to remember that civil authorities are 'sent by [God] to punish those who do evil and praise those who do good' (2:14). Government restrains much evil, despite the fact that some governments do much evil and even call evil good. The fact, however, that they are sent, providentially placed in governing office by God, also means that they are continually accountable to God. Every governing official will have to give answer to the Lord for how they fulfilled his charge. This gives context and comfort to us as we understand the place and role that God has given to earthly governments, and the relationship he calls us to have to them.

The Fruits and Freedom of Submission (2:15–17)

Honoring the Lord's command to submit to earthly governance for his sake, brings glory to him by our testimony. 'For this is God's will, that by doing good you should put to silence the ignorance of foolish people' (2:15). During the early church Christians were often slandered as being subversive to both government and society (Acts 21:27–28). While we may need to endure false accusations for a lifetime (Revelation 2:3) as our Lord Jesus Christ did (Isaiah 53:7–9), a submitted integrity to authority bears testimony to Christ which will convict and silence some in this life, and in time will bring all opponents to silence before God's throne.

A temptation facing Christians in Peter's day and since, is the idea that because Jesus Christ is Savior and King, we no longer need to submit to earthly powers and authorities. This call for "freedom" is really a call to pursue sin, self, and the establishment of some new earthly regime. Our Lord calls us to 'live as people who are free, not using your freedom as a cover-up for evil, but living as servants of God' (2:16). The freedom of forgiveness and new life with God in Christ produces holiness, making the Christian a growing servant of God in all areas of life, including submission with integrity to our governments. Too often as Christians, while we defend the freedom to worship and serve God, we chafe and grumble at the ordinances of human institutions, like taxes and speed limits. True freedom in Christ embraces his call to service and obedience.

This passage of God's Word to us concludes with a series of short imperatives: 'Honor everyone. Love the brotherhood. Fear God. Honor the emperor' (2:17). The integrity of our witness in society begins in the core of reverence towards God, and loving communion with God's people. But it must also push outwards to every area of life. As we understand that God is sovereign over all, that he is the one who has ordained government and the placement of every person in our lives, we can also live with confidence and intention that his grace is sufficient to enable us to walk in integrity towards all, with respect and submission that brings glory to him.

You and the Word

As you read verses 13–17 take note of the God-centeredness of this passage: "be subject for the Lord's sake .... [rulers] sent by him .... For this is the will of God ... living as servants of God ... Fear God." If there is one central theme which should deeply impact us from this passage it is this: if we are to honor civil authorities and their ordinances, giving them honor and respect in all areas where they do not command us to sin against God, then how much more ought we to honor and submit to God, giving him respect and reverence with great joy? "He changes times and seasons, he removes kings and sets up kings" (Daniel 2:21). There is no corruption, no slackness, no untimeliness in his rule over us. His governance is perfect in holiness, justice, goodness, love, mercy, and grace. His Son, our Savior, is anointed by him as Ruler over all. Isaiah prophesied:

> For to us a child is born, to us a son is given; and the government shall be upon his shoulder, and his name shall be called Wonderful Counselor, Mighty God, Everlasting Father, Prince of Peace. Of the increase of his government and of peace there will be no end, on the throne of David and over his kingdom, to establish it and uphold it with justice and with righteousness from this time forth and forevermore. The zeal of the LORD of hosts will do this. (Isaiah 9:6–7)

Attitude - World is Watching

Honor Everyone
Love Brotherhood
Fear God
Honor the Emperor (govt)

Tension - Navigate

12

Following in Jesus' Steps

Please read 1 Peter 2:18–25

Submitting to your employer (2:18–20)

For the early church in Asia Minor, slavery and servitude were everyday realities. Some people were slaves due to Rome's military conquests. Others were slaves or indentured servants because of outstanding debts or poverty. Slaves and servants performed a wide variety of tasks in society. Some were physical laborers for construction contractors; others lived their whole lives farming estates. Some were managers of estates, physicians, or teachers. Except for the very highest classes, everyone lived in some relationship of servitude to those above them. While our world seems different, the differences may well be more cosmetic than we realize. Most Christians today also work under the authority of employers; we have privacy and freedom to travel, but there are constraints on what we are able to do. For many in the global church, menial servitude and even slavery remain facts of life.

In this context Peter brings the Word of the risen Christ: 'Servants, be subject to your masters with all respect' (2:18). We are to obey the authority of those over us in our work with a genuine and complete respect. This does not mean that we can never voice a concern or give what we believe would be helpful input. It does mean that when we submit our opinion, we leave the decision-making that belongs to those above us respectfully to them. Where there is injustice, wrong-doing, we should pursue what is just and true—but that also is to be characterized by respect, following Scripture's patterns (cf. Matthew 18:15–20) including honoring civil laws. Being subject "with all respect" also means that our respect for work-place authority should not be confined to our workplaces. Many offer a semblance of respect that vanishes on lunch breaks with colleagues. It is easy to complain about a boss at home after a day's work. But we are called to a nobler and better life in Christ: a good test of true respect is whether or not it disappears in the absence of those over us.

What about injustice? (2:18–20)

God's Word challenges us to grow to completeness in glorifying him in this area of life. Our submission with all respect is to be 'not only to the good and gentle but also to the unjust' (2:18). It is usually easy for us to submit with heartfelt respect to a good and gentle employer: some bosses are great. But our respect cannot be limited by our employer's character. Peter covers the entire range of possibilities: "to the good ... but also to the unjust."

We need encouragement respecting hard employers, and Peter gives it to us: 'For this is a gracious thing, when, mindful of God, one endures sorrows while suffering unjustly' (2:19). This is the radical, counter-cultural call of new life in Christ: submitting with all respect and continuing in that respectful submission while suffering under the injustice of an earthly master. You see, when injustice happens to us, we often act as though it is a great calamity. We are outraged because we are suffering unjustly, and it is soon hard to find a shred of respectful submission left. What pleases God, though, is when by his grace we "bear up" under this burden, trusting him with patient endurance as we continue in a walk of respectful integrity.

Physical punishment, including beatings, hunger, and exposure, were standard for many slaves and servants in the Roman Empire. Peter reminds the readers, which included Christian slaves, that there is no honor in suffering because of our sin: 'for what credit is it if, when you sin and are beaten for it, you endure?' (2:20). There is nothing noble in not complaining when we get discipline that we deserve. 'But if when you do good and suffer for it you endure, this is a gracious thing in the sight of God' (2:20). Peter reaffirms that patient endurance through unjust suffering, even where it is *because* we have done what is good, is a beautiful testimony to God's glory. It is perhaps the highest expression of integrity of respectful obedience. Today there is often the possibility of leaving an unjust employer; but, as in Peter's day, leaving is not always an option. Yet, whether our situation is changeable or permanent, our calling through it is the same: do good, and endure in doing good for God's glory.

Following Christ's example (2:21–23)

Having exhorted us, Peter turns our attention to Jesus: 'For to this you have been called, because Christ also suffered for you, leaving you an example, so that you might follow in his steps' (2:21). Our Lord Jesus not only suffered for us in the great exchange of redemption, but also willingly suffered to be able to leave us the perfect example of living the way God intended. As he lived out his calling in the midst of a sinful world, our Lord 'committed no sin, neither was deceit found in his mouth. When he was reviled, he did not revile in return; when he suffered, he did not threaten, but continued entrusting himself to him who judges justly' (2:22–23). As he went through the suffering of injustice for us, Jesus did not respond in kind. Rather, he entrusted himself fully to the Father's perfect justice, continuing to walk in perfect goodness and truth. In doing all of this our Lord Jesus Christ glorified the Father, magnified the law, and fulfilled all righteousness in a self-loving, God hating world.

Jesus is the perfect and complete embodiment of God's law. The way Jesus lived with the fullness of respect and submission to earthly authorities is what God expects of us every work day. Christ's example is exactly what we are called to: a genuine and holistic respect and submission, even through injustice. This is convicting: not only do we not fulfill what we are called to; we often do the exact opposite.

Jesus, the Perfect Savior (2:24–25)

Even as we become aware of the depth and frequency of our violations of God's call to pursue respectful submission, Peter reaffirms to us Christ's perfect sufficiency as the One who saves us from our sin. 'Christ also suffered for you ... He himself bore our sins in his body on the tree, that we might die to sin and live to righteousness' (2:21, 24).

Theologians often speak of Christ's "active" and "passive" obedience in his great work of the atonement. Passive obedience describes Jesus' willing taking to himself the penalty and punishment due for our sin. This was the great sacrifice of his suffering unto death on the cross: his body broken, his blood shed as a complete payment for the sin of his people. Jesus' active obedience is his complete fulfillment of the obedience we are called to. He fulfilled all righteousness. Jesus both completely lived the law's precepts, and completely paid the penalty due to his people for breaking the law of God.

As we come to him in faith and repentance, both Jesus' active and passive obedience are accounted to us so that the Christian is not only forgiven, but also stands clothed in Christ's righteousness. 'By his wounds you have been healed' (2:24). The Christian is united to Christ, under his care, and empowered to new life. This immense totality is what we freely receive by faith in Christ. 'For you were straying like sheep, but have now returned to the Shepherd and Overseer of your souls' (2:25).

The more we understand the fullness of who Jesus is and what he has done and does do, the more our hearts are filled with love and the desire to give our lives to following our Savior. Rather than viewing the call to be subject to our masters with all respect as an impossible burden, it becomes our freedom and joy to pursue this kind of a workplace life in love for God, and our neighbor. Christ is completely sufficient for us: he is our "wisdom, righteousness, sanctification and redemption" (1 Corinthians 1:30). Everything is answered in him. As we live this new life in Christ, we become living pictures of the gospel of Christ at work.

You and the Word

Who are your workplace superiors? Consider your relationship with those to whom you are accountable in the varied aspects of your life calling. How can you grow to a greater maturity in Christ and a more complete life of loving gratitude to him in your working relationships? Pray that God would give you a clear self-awareness in the light of his Word. Ask him to forgive your sin. Ask him to enable you to pursue substantial, steady growth in holiness in a life of respectful workplace integrity, to his glory.

> May the mind of Christ my Savior live in me from day to day,
> By his love and pow'r controlling all I do and say.

May the Word of God dwell richly in my heart from hour to hour,
So that all may see I triumph only through his pow'r.[1]

13

Christ-like Wives and Husbands

Please read 1 Peter 3:1–7

The pursuit of godly submission (3:1–2)

The theme of proclaiming God's excellencies through daily living continues in the third chapter of the epistle. From civic and workplace callings, Peter moves on to marriage relationships: 'Likewise, wives, be subject to your own husbands' (3:1). The language in verse 1 is an immediate parallel to that in verses 13 and 18 of chapter 2. It reminds us that, just as for Jesus, respectful submission will be a holistic characteristic of the Christian, displayed in every circumstance where God has ordained a relationship of leadership or authority.

God's Word clearly defines the parameters in each case: just as servants are only under the authority of their own masters, and citizens to their own governments, wives are to be subject only to their own husbands. Women in general are not subject to men in general. What does it mean to be subject to your own husband, as a wife? While Scripture has much else to say about the marriage relationship (cf. Ephesians 5:22–33), the calling Peter addresses here is for wives to follow and support their husbands in all things that are in harmony with God's Word.

The call for a wife to submit to her husband is never a call to submit to or condone sin in any form. Nor does it negate the scriptural freedom for a wife to divorce her husband where he has broken the marriage covenant through adultery, abuse, or desertion. Neither does submission imply inferiority or lesser worth. It does mean that in lawful things, a wife is to treat her husband as the leader in the relationship, not because of inherent superiority, but because of created roles.

Peter impresses the completeness of this call, noting that it applies even to the Christian wife of an unbelieving husband: 'so that even if some do not obey the word, they may be won without a word by the conduct of their wives' (3:1). In the early church, having a husband who did not obey the word was not unusual. The church was growing rapidly through gospel witness and some wives had husbands who converted later or not at all. Through the proclamation of the Word, men and women were being saved, but salvation did not necessarily mean change in the immediate context of life.

Peter tenderly encourages his readers, living in a pre-Christian world, that the faithful testimony of a godly wife may be the means that the Holy Spirit uses to bring the Word to triumph in his life. 'When they see your respectful and pure conduct' (3:2), so different from the bitterness, anger, and promiscuity common to the culture, people will be convicted by its holiness.

The pursuit of unfading beauty (3:3–5)

Much like ours, Greco-Roman and Near Eastern culture was obsessed with physical beauty. Our society, like theirs, idolizes outward beauty and even disparages those whose outward beauty is in decline. Natural beauty is no longer enough; even make-up artists have become basic. Now, images are airbrushed and adjusted, bodies are modified through injections and surgeries. The sad consequences, from inability to breastfeed to eating disorders, are all around us. Surrounded by unrealistic standards, many women feel unattractive. This spiritual danger, at best a distraction, at worst idolatry, is what Peter now turns to address: 'Do not let your adorning be external—the braiding of hair and the putting on of gold jewelry, or the clothing you wear—but let your adorning be the hidden person of the heart with the imperishable beauty of a gentle and quiet spirit, which in God's sight is very precious' (3:3–4).

The call to transfer our priority of concern and energy from outer beauty to inner beauty is not a rejection of outward beauty. Scripture reminds us that God created physical beauty (cf. Song of Solomon 1:10–13; Ezekiel 16:6–14; Revelation 21:2). Outward beauty and adornment are God's gifts, so we can be thankful for and enjoy them. But Peter reorients us, freeing us from our propensity to pursue physical beauty sinfully. He focuses us on the pursuit of lasting beauty: beauty that shines through a person, from the inside out.

The apostle focuses on two aspects of character: gentleness and quietness of spirit, or contented peace in God, as the positive characteristics God desires in a wife. These characteristics are not a call to reclusive timidity: one can be gentle and content in Christ, while at the same time being direct, zealous, and outgoing. They are rather the opposites of the harsh anger and anxiety which naturally flow from sinful hearts. God values a gentle and quiet spirit tremendously. It is very precious to him—so precious that he sent his Son to save us from the sins of the idolatry of outer appearance, harshness, and anxiety, to a new life of beauty and peace.

Gentleness and quietness of spirit makes a person a beautiful person, whether she is 20, 40, or 85. This is "the imperishable beauty" that triumphs over the present curse of decay and death, anticipating the day of resurrection. Then, our perishable, fading bodies will be brought into the fullness of new life, in perfect beauty that will never fade.

The pursuit of confident faith (3:6)

Peter explains that 'this is how the holy women who hoped in God used to adorn themselves, by submitting to their own husbands' (3:6). We have a specific example of a wife who pursued a submitted, gentle, life in Christ: 'Sarah obeyed Abraham calling him lord' (3:6). We know that Sarah was a woman of significant outward beauty (cf. Genesis 12:10–14). Yet what is noteworthy about her is the beauty of her submission and respect, through faith in Christ, to Abraham. Peter tells us that we are her children, 'if you do good and do not fear anything that is frightening' (3:6).

The call to submit, pursuing good, without giving way to fear is eminently practical. Undoubtedly, through her nomadic, sometimes dangerous life, Sarah would have wondered where her husband's decisions might lead. Some of Abraham's decisions were sinful (Genesis 12:10–20; 20:1–18). While we do not have record of Sarah counselling him to the contrary in these situations, we do see that the Lord was faithful in delivering her, even from her own sin (Genesis 18:13–15; 21:5–7). Scripture's testimony is that God's grace was sufficient to forgive Sarah, enable her to walk in faith in him (Hebrews 11:11), living as an excellent wife in her relationship to her husband (Proverbs 31:10–12). Submission to another sinner can make us fear; God tells us that we do not need to when we submit out of love for Christ, trusting in his preserving grace.

A word to husbands (3:7)

The apostle has called wives to follow Sarah's example, looking to Jesus's grace to grow in true beauty and holy respect. Now he addresses husbands. 'Likewise, husbands, live with you wives in an understanding way, showing honor to the woman as the weaker vessel' (3:7).

Just as God is the one who has placed the husband in the role of leadership, God is the one who defines what this leadership is. Verse 7 tells us that the husband is to be characterized by being considerate and understanding as he leads. This requires intentional care in nurturing good communication; ordinarily, decisions will come through husband-wife consensus. While good communication and healthy decision-making are necessary, being understanding as a husband foundationally requires a spirit of loving self-sacrifice: putting your wife's needs and cares before your own. We can only attain this as we receive grace and live life in Christ, as Peter's opening word "likewise" (3:7) reminds us.

The husband is also to honor and respect his wife, including understanding that she is physically and emotionally different from himself, a distinction described here by God's Word as being "weaker" (3:7). How a Christian husband responds to this relational calling to understand and honor his wife will directly impact his spiritual vitality and the spiritual health of his household. Why? Because God cares for his children. They are precious to him, and he will not prosper husbands who are abusing or neglecting their wives, since they are 'heirs with you of the grace of life' (3:7). God does not listen to Christian men who knowingly misrepresent Christ's sacrificial, loving example (3:7). Husbands, you are to earnestly pursue this aspect of your new life in Christ 'so that your prayers may not be hindered' (3:7).

You and the Word

Our closest relationships are usually the places where the sinful tendencies of our hearts are most often exposed. This means that marriage is an area of life in which we can grow profoundly deeper and stronger as his new creation. Sanctification in marriage has the ripple effect of helping our sanctification in other areas of life. Our Lord has given you wisdom and instruction here by his Word, and promises his grace and Spirit as you rely on him. Live the calling he gives, and encourage others around you to do so, to his glory, for his delight.

"I am my beloved's, and my beloved is mine ..." (Song of Solomon 6:3)

God's Calling for All of Us

Please read 1 Peter 3:8–12

The Character of the Christian (3:8)

From the opening of this epistle, Peter has declared the great realities of God's gospel to us, and then applied it to the varied life relationships we find ourselves in as citizens, employees, and spouses. As a final conclusion to these applications, Peter now brings our attention to our calling in Christ as members of his church—'all of you' (3:8)—in this present world. How are we to relate to each other, as fellow Christians? How are we to relate to others around us?

First, we are to have 'unity of mind' (3:8). Some translations state, "be harmonious," which also captures the meaning of the text. As fellow Christians—each deserving justice but purchased by the blood of the same Savior and Lord Jesus Christ, sharing the same hope of glory—how could we be at peace with anything less than a growing unity of mind with each other?

God wants his people to live in harmony because he is the God of perfect unity and harmony: Father, Son and Holy Spirit.

Second, we are to have 'sympathy' for one another (3:8). If our hearts are unmoved by the struggles and sufferings of others, there is something drastically wrong with us. To be cold and untouched in the midst of sin, brokenness, and suffering is really a denial that we are followers of Christ. Our God is moved with compassion for us. Scripture displays this to us over and over. In the gospels we see Jesus weeping at the tomb of Lazarus (John 11:35), weeping over the cities that refused to repent (Matthew 23:17), We see the ultimate display of his sympathy in his compassion for us at the cross, where he entered the depths of suffering for our salvation (Hebrews 2:9–18).

Third, we are to have 'brotherly love' for each other (3:8). As individual Christians making up the body of the church, we are not merely friends, but family. Hebrews tells us that the Father is "bringing many sons to glory" through his Son. This is why the author goes on to tell us, "he is not ashamed to call them brothers, saying I will tell of your name to my brothers; in the midst of the congregation I will sing your praise" (Hebrews 2:10–12). Since we are brought into the God's family through his great love, so we are to take great joy in loving each other.

Fourth, we are to have a 'tender heart' towards each other (3:8). Again, this is because of who God is. Our Lord has been incredibly tender, kind hearted towards us as a sinful people. Where our hearts were bent in hatred against him, he changed us, brought us to himself, cleansed, and renews us. He knows our weakness and struggles as his creatures, and he is kind towards us (Isaiah 42:2–3).

Finally, the Lord, through Peter, calls us to have 'a humble mind' (3:8). Humility is the positive opposite to pride. It is displayed in the willingness to serve others, including where that means self-sacrifice. It does not draw attention to ourselves, but to the grace, goodness, and glory of God. The greatest example of humility is found in our Lord Jesus Christ, "who, though he was in the form of God, did not count equality with God a thing to be grasped, but made himself nothing, taking the form of a servant, being born in the likeness of men. And being found in human form, he humbled himself by becoming obedient to the point of death, even death on a cross" (Philippians 2:6–8).

Good, Not Evil (3:9–11)

Where these fruits of the Spirit are growing characteristics in our lives, our actions will be transformed. The man, woman, or child, who knows and lives in Christ with sympathy, brotherly love, a tender heart, and a humble mind will embrace the ensuing imperative: 'Do not repay evil for evil, or reviling for reviling, but on the contrary, bless' (3:9).

Our old nature responds in kind when we are insulted or injured. We are called to the opposite: Calvin says that, "evils are to be overcome by acts of kindness ... we ought to imitate in this case our heavenly Father, who makes his sun to rise on the unworthy."[1] God daily endures innumerable insults and evils against himself and "he is patient toward you, not wishing that any should perish" (2 Peter 3:9). When Jesus "was reviled, he did not revile in return; when he suffered, he did not threaten, but kept on entrusting himself to him who judges justly" (2:23). He prayed, "Father, forgive them, for they know not what they do" (Luke 23:34).

By God's grace in Christ, we are enabled to follow Jesus in blessing instead of cursing, just as Stephen did to his murderers: "Lord, do not hold this sin against them" (Acts 7:60). Most of us will never face evil to the point of our martyrdom, but if we do, here is testimony that God's grace is sufficient for us to finish well even in the face of the greatest evils. This how we are called to live, and die: 'for to this you were called, that you may obtain a blessing' (3:9).

Peter amplifies his exhortation to us as he cites Psalm 34: 'For whoever desires to love life and see good days, let him keep his tongue from speaking evil, and his lips from speaking deceit; let him turn away from evil and do good; let him seek peace and pursue it' (3:10–11). Do you want to love life and see good days? Then follow Christ in rejecting evil. By his strength put your sin to death and pursue good instead. You will experience goodness now already, even in trials and suffering, and the eternal fullness of life and good days to come.

Always Before God (3:12)

Peter's citation of Psalm 34 concludes with the Lord's reminder that he is watching us, sees us, and knows us. Nothing is hidden from his sight. He knows everything past, present, and future. Every moment we live before his face. There is amazing comfort here for Christians: 'the eyes of the Lord are on the righteous, and his ears are open to their prayer' (3:12). As we war against our remaining sin and face the hostility of a world that loves sin, he wants us to know that he lovingly watches over us. Where human fathers attentively watch over their children, protecting them, listening to them, and enjoying their company, the Lord does this with perfect love and wisdom. The comfort for God's children concludes with a warning to those who continue to pursue evil: 'but the face of the Lord is against those who do evil' (3:12). God is fully aware of everyone, not only his children. If your life is marked by the pursuit of what God says is evil, then he is against you. You are living in an untenable, futile rebellion. The day of his judgment against you is steadily approaching. Unless you obey his call to repent and come to his Son in faith, you remain in this dangerous place with a terrifying reality ahead (Psalm 2:12). This sober reality is comforting for

Christians: Christ the King will subdue all his and our enemies. He knows our struggles and sufferings, and is bringing our salvation to completion.

You and the Word

1 Peter 3:8–12 calls us to embrace the fullness of new life in Christ, putting to death the sin that remains in us. This call impacts every area of life, including our relationships. Prayerfully consider how you can grow in, "unity of mind, sympathy, brotherly love, a tender heart, and a humble mind" towards those around you. When and where can you bless, instead of returning evil for evil? Where in your life and relationships can you turn from evil and do good, seeking peace and pursuing it? Pursue these things looking to Jesus. He is sufficient for you in this. He cares for us with complete and constant attentiveness (3:12).

> O Church, arise, and put your armor on,
> Hear the call of Christ our captain
> For now the weak can say that they are strong
> In the strength that God has given.[2]

15

Living for Christ: Fearless, Ready, and Good

Please read 1 Peter 3:13–17

Fearless (3:13–14)

Fear influences us more than we realize. The same has been true for Christians through the centuries, including in the churches of Asia Minor during Peter's ministry. How often aren't we tempted to pull back on being zealous for what is good—including proclaiming the excellencies of the God who has saved us? We fear what people might do to us—or think of us—as a result. The Word addresses our fears by opening our eyes to the fact that we live and move and have our being in God's presence. Peter has just reminded us that "the eyes of the Lord are on the righteous" but "the face of the Lord is against those who do evil" (3:12). This makes the next question rhetorical: 'Now who is there to harm you if you are zealous for what is good?' (3:13)

Throughout the Bible, God tells us that he cares perfectly for us. He reminds us that he sovereignly works all things together for our good. Peter's question echoes Paul's in Romans 8: "If God is for us, who can be against us?" (Romans 8:31) When we know that God is for our faithfulness, we experience freedom and boldness in serving him.

In asking, "who is there to harm you?" Peter is not glibly ignoring the reality of persecution and hardship on account of zeal for what is good. He gives opportunity for us to consider who might harm us—and opens our eyes to the presence of the majesty and power of God, before whose face we, and they, live. Peter's response doubly answers and completes the point: 'But even if you should suffer for righteousness sake, you will be blessed' (3:14).

God never minimizes the reality of suffering. Instead, the Word reaffirms to us that following Christ through suffering is neither triumph for evil nor a futile experience for the Christian. It is the persecutor who acts in sheer folly and futility against the Lord and his people (cf. Psalm 2), while sufferings are turned to blessing for the children of God. The conclusion? Peter cites the Lord's charge to Isaiah (Isaiah 8:12): 'Have no fear of them, nor be troubled, but in your hearts honor Christ the Lord as holy' (3:14–15). By looking to Jesus and honoring him internally, we are enabled to be increasingly fearless in his service.

Honoring Christ begins with our awareness that he willingly went through humiliation and suffering to death, so that we might be brought from death to life and exalted with him (cf. Ephesians 2:1–10; Hebrews 2:9–13; 1 Peter 2:9–10). It is only fitting that we focus on exalting him by pursuing willing submission, starting at the core of our being. He is to be the Lord of our hearts, of all our desires, motives, and affections. To honor Christ in our hearts is to take up his call and promise: "You shall be holy, for I am holy" (1 Peter 1:16).

Ready (3:15)

Understanding life in God's presence means that our fears of what men might do to us begin to wane as our confidence in him rises. And so Peter calls us to a specific way that we can "honor Christ the Lord as holy" in our hearts (3:15). It is by 'always being prepared to make a defense to anyone who asks you for a reason for the hope that is in you' (3:15). The radical opposite to being silenced by fear is being ready to speak of Christ, honoring him in doing so. The grammar of the text connects this readiness not only to our awareness of God's presence (3:12), but also to sanctifying Christ as Lord in our hearts. When we are living to exalt Christ in our personal lives, we will find we are most ready to speak to others of him. A life of growing holiness in love for Christ will intrigue and challenge those apart from Christ, leading them to ask why we live the way we do. (3:15) At the same time, as we exalt Christ in our lives, pursuing complete holiness to the Lord (Exodus 28:36), we are also best prepared to share the reason for the hope that we have.

Good (3:15–17)

The manner in which we defend and declare the reason for our hope in the Triune God is what Peter now draws our attention to. Questions about our lives from a world at enmity with God will not necessarily be friendly questions. The subtlety of our own remaining sin means that we can be prone to harshness in response to those who question our hope in Christ. Not only are we to not fear critics of life in Christ, but in answering them, we are also to 'do it with gentleness and respect, having a good conscience, so that, when you are slandered, those who revile your good behavior in Christ may be put to shame' (3:15–16). Our good behavior in Christ is displayed not only by our answer, but also our manner of answering. This is how we holistically point a hostile culture to Christ.

Gentleness and respect in our answers, while bearing the powerful Word, may well bear fruit to salvation in others. It will put to shame those who slander and revile the evident goodness of life in Christ. In God's wise providence, however, just as in Jesus's earthly ministry, faithfulness may mean continued suffering.

And so Peter appends another reason to pursue a holistic Christ honoring life in a hostile culture: 'For it is better to suffer for doing good, if that should be God's will, than for doing evil' (3:17). His words here are almost identical to the earlier address to servants and slaves, and will be repeated again later (1 Peter 2:20; 4:14–16). In these cases they are intimately linked to the reality that where we suffer for doing good we are actually sharing in Christ's sufferings. This is both a great honor and cause for rejoicing: now and even more so when his glory is revealed (1 Peter 4:13).

You and the Word

In what ways does the fear of man squeeze and shrink your zealous pursuit of new life in Christ? Are you capitulating to this world's efforts to mute what might otherwise be a bold and loving testimony to the truth of God and his Word? If you are like me, prayerfully listening to God's Word in 1 Peter 3:13–17 encourages and convicts you at the same time. Where the Spirit convicts you of sin, exposing your failures and weakness, he also graciously directs you to Christ, "who suffered once for sins, the righteous for the unrighteous" (1 Peter 3:18). Give thanks that by the grace of your Lord and Savior you can both receive forgiveness and grow in honoring him in your life and conversation, despite opposition. Through Christ who strengthens you, Isaiah's words can be the increasing testimony of your life:

> I will greatly rejoice in the LORD;

My soul shall exult in my God,
For he has clothed me with the garments of salvation;
He has covered me with the robes of righteousness ...

For Zion's sake I will not keep silent,
And for Jerusalem's sake I will not be quiet,
Until her righteousness goes forth as brightness,
And her salvation as a burning torch. (Isaiah 61:10, 62:1)

16

Encouragements to Faithfulness

Please read 1 Peter 3:18–22

Christ also suffered (3:18)

How can we continue to grow in being zealous for what is good? How can we live fearlessly, ready to proclaim the excellencies of God, even while we anticipate the real possibility of suffering for it? That comes when we begin to realize that "we who are saved suffer and are blessed because Christ suffered and was glorified as our Savior."[1]

Peter directs us to consider Jesus: 'For Christ also suffered once for sins, the righteous for the unrighteous, that he might bring us to God, being put to death in the flesh, but made alive in the spirit' (3:18). Christ suffered for our sins, so that we, who are sinners, can be reconciled to God. His suffering and death was a purposeful, sufficient atonement, satisfying the justice, penalty, and wrath we deserve from God. The Greek term translated "once" implies in this context that his suffering was once for all: it never needs to be repeated (cf. Hebrews 10:10–14). Jesus's sufferings and death were substitutionary. He took our place; the innocent for the guilty, the just for the unjust. This was necessary to restore us to God. Christ suffered to the extent of being put to death but death had no hold on him. He was raised bodily in the spirit, exalted to resurrection glory by the power of the Godhead (cf. Galatians 1:1; John 10:18).

When our real or imagined sufferings for his sake are placed in the light of Jesus's far greater, redeeming suffering for us, the darkness of our fear is answered. What greater joy can we have than to follow our Savior, bearing his Word to others, patiently enduring sufferings over which he is sovereign? We glorify him as we do and he delights in our loving faithfulness to him: "Blessed are you when others revile you and persecute you and utter all kinds of evil against you falsely on my account. Rejoice and be glad, for your reward is great in heaven ..." (Matthew 5:11).

The Word is vindicated (3:19–20)

A second great encouragement flows from the apostle's pen as the Spirit directs him to point us to Jesus. God's Word is always vindicated, because he is God. He vindicated the proclamation of his Word by his prophets throughout the Old Testament; he vindicated the only begotten Son, the Word made flesh; and he vindicates the subsequent New Testament era proclamation of his Word, including the life witness of his people to his Word. From verse 18 into verses 19 and 20, Peter directs our focus back to an early example of this in Genesis. We read that Christ was made alive in the spirit, 'in which he went and proclaimed to the spirits in prison because they formerly did not obey, when God's patience waited in the days of Noah, while the ark was being prepared, in which a few, that is, eight persons, were brought safely through water' (3:18–20).

Just as the eternal Son saved and transformed Peter, Stephen, and others, making them proclaimers of his gospel, so Christ, long before his incarnation, transformed Noah spiritually

(Hebrews 13:8). He equipped and moved Noah to preach his Word while building the ark.

Why does Peter raise this example? Not only to show us the unity of Scripture and Christ's saving work through history, but also to remind us that the Word for which we suffer, the Christ for whom we suffer, will vindicate us. Noah was the laughing stock of his generation. Still, he listened to and obeyed God's gracious warning and invitation (Psalm 2). His faith and preaching were massively vindicated in his own family's salvation and in the flood that brought death and judgement to the rest of humanity. His warning and invitation to safety proved perfectly accurate and true. Christ himself spoke through Noah.

Note how Scripture describes Noah's contemporaries who heard the proclamation of Christ: they are 'the spirits in prison ... [who] formerly did not obey' (3:19–20). Every single individual of the days leading up to the flood, with the exception of Noah and his family, died in that flood and is now under the wrath of God in hell. They are now in a prison from which there is no escape. Once disobedient, their rebellion has been entirely crushed. God has highly exalted Christ, "so that at the name of Jesus every knee should bow, in heaven and on earth and under the earth, and every tongue confess that Jesus Christ is Lord, to the glory of God the Father" (Philippians 2:10; Romans 14:10–12). For them, there is no longer the suppression of truth in unrighteousness, but only the fearful expectation of further judgment (Hebrews 10:26). They exist in sober contrast to the gracious deliverance of Noah and his family whom God brought safely through the flood waters.

Christ's victory is your salvation (3:21–22)

Peter's final encouragement to us in this chapter draws a parallel between the deliverance of Noah and his family "safely through water" (3:20) and baptism: 'Baptism which corresponds to this, now saves you, not as a removal of dirt from the body but as an appeal to God for a good conscience, through the resurrection of Jesus Christ, who has gone into heaven and is at the right hand of God, with angels, authorities, and powers having been subjected to him' (3:21–22). A hasty reading of these verses might lead us to think that baptism saves us. But the whole of the text makes it clear that what is in view is our baptism as it is confirmed by our faith in Jesus Christ. Peter states it is not the water of baptism that saves us by cleansing us; rather, we are saved as we are baptized and appeal to God for a good conscience. This is true both for baptized infants of believers, as well as for those baptized on their conversion. As we take hold of the gospel promises proclaimed and sealed to us in our baptism, we receive forgiveness of sins and the imputation of the righteousness that Christ alone can give. Then, through Jesus' blood, we draw near to God "in full assurance of faith, with our hearts sprinkled clean from an evil conscience and our bodies washed with pure water" (Hebrews 10:22).

Our salvation is found in Christ. While God delivered Noah and his family from the flood through the ark, it is 'through the resurrection Christ' (3:21) that we and they are saved from the judgement that we deserve. Christ's perfect righteousness, complete atonement, and saving power are vindicated in his resurrection. He is the one 'who has gone into heaven and is at the right hand of God, with angels, authorities, and powers having been subjected to him' (3:22). Enthroned as the King over all creation, Christ governs everything for our salvation. Satan and his demons, angels, emperors, dictators, presidents, governments, judges, tribunals, police, criminals, terrorists, our co-workers and neighbors, only live and move and have their being by his sovereign will. Christ is the living seal of every promise of God's Word to us. There is no greater comfort than to know that the eternal Son made flesh, who suffered, died, and is risen and ascended, is calling us through suffering to blessing.

You and the Word

Our Lord knows the timidity and fear many of us have as a result of our own small mindedness and the sin of those around us. He knows that this world is opposed to him and to us as his children. He knows our counter-factual tendency to see people as big and himself as small and distant. He graciously speaks to us by his Word, reminding us of who he is, and what he is doing, to deliver us from the shackles we, and the world, try to place on zeal for what is good.

> Now may the God of peace
> who brought again from the dead our Lord Jesus,
> The great shepherd of the sheep,
> by the blood of the eternal covenant,
> Equip you with everything good that you may do his will,
> Working in us that which is pleasing in his sight,
> Through Jesus Christ, to whom be glory,
> forever and ever. Amen. (Hebrews 13:20–21)

17

United to Christ, Living for God

Please read 1 Peter 4:1–11

United to Christ in his sufferings and death (4:1–2)

One of the great themes of the first epistle of Peter is holiness (1 Peter 1:15–16). Peter begins the fourth chapter by reminding us again that the call to pursue holiness unto the Lord through suffering, is rooted in Jesus's person and work: 'Since therefore Christ suffered in the flesh, arm yourselves with the same way of thinking' (4:1). Christ, the sinless One, suffered for our salvation; he suffered in our place. His delight and determination was to pursue holiness in all things, laying down his life in substitutionary sacrifice for us, out of love for the Father, and love for us. He knew the suffering this entailed: "Now is my soul troubled. And what shall I say? Father, save me from this hour? But for this purpose I have come to this hour. Father, glorify your name" (John 12:27–28). Christ pursued his calling to the full, until he could declare, "It is finished" (John 19:30).

Jesus mindset, Peter tells us, is the paradigm for us. We are to arm ourselves with the same way of thinking, anticipating that in some measure, we will suffer for righteousness' sake. We need to consider it well worth the cost to glorify our Redeemer (Matthew 5:10–12; John 15:20). Not only is Jesus well worth suffering for, but as we consider his sufferings and victory through them for our salvation, we are also further armed against temptations to sin.

Peter adds to the call to take up Christ's mindset a reminder of the reality of the spiritual transformation made evident in willingness to suffer in following him: 'for whoever has suffered in the flesh has ceased from sin, so as to live for the rest of the time in the flesh no longer for human passions but for the will of God' (4:1–2). There is strong confidence in the text here. When we suffer for Christ and his cause, we can be assured that we "are dead to sin, and alive to God in Christ Jesus" (Romans 6:11). This does not mean there is no further battle to engage against our own remaining sin—Peter encourages us in the pursuit of holiness. But it does mean there has been a fundamental change. "We who were dead in trespasses and sins have been made alive together with Christ" (Ephesians 2:1–10). United to him by grace through faith, our desire now is like Christ's: "not my will, but yours, be done" (Luke 22:42).

Leaving the old life (4:3–5)

Reflecting on the past of the believers in Asia Minor, Peter reminds the church that they are to live the rest of their lives for God. 'For the time that is past suffices for doing what the Gentiles want to do, living in sensuality, passions, drunkenness, orgies, drinking parties, and lawless idolatry' (4:3). These are ancient patterns of rebellion against God and his goodness. Living in them is what people want to do apart from Christ, and have since the fall. This is what we desired and did before our own salvation (Romans 3:11–12). Peter exhorts us to not turn back to wasting our lives in sin against the Lord; we have already wasted enough of our lives that way.

He also reminds the church to be aware that the refusal to pursue sin and instead pursue holiness, exposes the darkness of friends, family, and communities who remain in love with sin. It causes discomfort and anger. 'With respect to this they are surprised when you do not join them in the same flood of debauchery, and they malign you' (4:4) The surprise that non-Christians feel when they see someone's life is not a pleasant surprise, neither is its fruit. The Greek word "blaspheme" translated here as, "they malign you," can also be literally translated, "they heap abuse on you"—a common theme in the life of believers in the church of Asia Minor[1] (2:12, 15; 3:9, 16). Charles Spurgeon remarks, "what a strange world this is! It speaks evil of men because they will not do evil!"[2] Peter's statement of this hard reality of unjust suffering comes with pastoral tenderness—Christ's word to his beloved church. Though the world despises us, the apostle reassures us that our Lord is on our side. Both Christians and the world opposed to Christ exist under God's sovereign and holy rule. They presently malign the bride of Christ, 'but they will give account to him who is ready to judge the living and the dead' (4:5).

The awesome reality of impending judgment by the Lord is reason to proclaim salvation: 'For this is why the gospel was preached even to those who are dead, that though judged in the flesh the way people are, they might live in the spirit the way God does' (4:6). Peter has in view the history of redemption going back through the Old Testament. God is holy. He is just and justifier (Romans 3:26). In love, he purposed from eternity past to save a people from fallen, rebel humanity by the Son. Through the history of this world he uses the foolishness of preaching as his powerful means to save sinners (1 Corinthians

1:18–31). While those redeemed by his grace were and are, "strangers and exiles on the earth," they have been transformed to life with God, who is "not ashamed to be called their God" (Hebrews 10:13, 16). Though pagans judge them as evil, they are Christ's, and are holy in him. In Jesus Christ God has judged otherwise.

Living the new life (4:7–11)

Both the Lord's gracious salvation and his imminent return are in mind as Peter exhorts us to steadfastness in new life. 'The end of all things is at hand; therefore be self-controlled and sober-minded for the sake of your prayers' (4:7) The awareness of Christ's approaching return motivates not only to courage in the face of opposition, but also to a faithful godliness. Through Christ, the Christian has "put off the old self with its practices" and "put on the new self, which is being renewed after the image of its creator" (Colossians 3:9–10). Peter exhorts the church to continued growth in new life in Christ, which includes guarding our desires and actions, living with clear awareness of both who God is and the fact that we live and move and have our being in him (Acts 17:28). Self-control and sober-mindedness "equip us for prayer," enabling close communion with our Lord.[3]

The anticipation of Christ's return should also spur us to greater zeal for our life together as his body. Suffering can make us turn inward and sin divides. So Peter exhorts us to minister to one another. 'Above all, keep loving one another earnestly, since love covers a multitude of sins. Show hospitality without grumbling. As each one has received a gift, use it to serve one another as good stewards of God's varied grace' (4:8–10). Instead of being unforgiving to the repentant, grumbling about the needy, and self-serving, the church is to be epitomized by earnest love, generous hospitality, and the intentional use of varied gifts for mutual service. Because this reflects the very being and character of the God of grace, it brings blessing.

Peter gives two categories of gifts in the church, along with the manner in which these gifts, received from the Lord, should be exercised: 'whoever speaks, as one who speaks oracles of God; whoever serves, as one who serves by the strength God supplies' (4:11). While there is a general application here for the speaking and service of every believer, the office bearers are particularly in view. Pastors called to preach and teach in the church are to do so, "reverently in God's fear and sincerity ... as ministering God's Word and not [their] own."[4] They are to be profoundly aware of the sacred majesty of God's Word.[5] They are to preach in a way that makes it plain that God speaks by his Word. Both the content and delivery of their addresses must reflect this. Ministers of the Word must be aware and clear that they are under the authority of the Word of God and the God of the Word. As deacons serve the needs of Christ's church, they are to do so knowing that their service is only by the strength of God, who works in us, "both to will and to work for his good pleasure" (Philippians 2:13). Humility, reliance on the Lord, and expectancy that he will "supply every need" should characterize their ministry (Philippians 4:19).

Why are those who speak and serve to use their God-given gifts in this way? 'In order that in everything God may be glorified through Christ Jesus' (4:11). Preaching and serving others, whether by lay people or ordained servants in their particular callings, is not about the individual who ministers. In its motivation, content, and purpose, genuine ministry is about God's glory: returning our all to him who has given us all things in Christ Jesus. 'To him belong glory and dominion forever and ever. Amen.' (4:11)

You and the Word

In the first part of this chapter, Peter calls us to look to Jesus, put sin to death, and willingly follow our Savior in the earthly suffering that comes through the world's animosity (v. 1–11). Just as Jesus did, entrust yourself to the Father in doing good. He is faithful and just; he is ready to judge. As you anticipate Christ's return, pursue the beauty of holiness in his church, exercising the gifts and calling the Lord has given you to serve him and others. Pray for and love your fellow believers. Pursue growth in showing generous and cheerful hospitality, serving others with your gifts. Ask your Lord and Savior to help you love and glorify him; he is sufficient to enable you to grow in what he calls you to (2 Corinthians 3:5). He is worthy of your all (Revelation 5:12).

The church's one Foundation
Is Jesus Christ her Lord;
She is his new creation
By water and the Word:
From heav'n he came and sought her
To be his holy bride;
With his own blood he bought her,
And for her life he died.

Elect from ev'ry nation,
Yet one o'er all the earth,
Her charter of salvation
One Lord, one faith, one birth;
One holy Name she blesses,
Partakes one holy food.
And to one hope she presses,
With ev'ry grace endued.

'Mid toil and tribulation,
And tumult of her war,
She waits the consummation

Of peace for evermore;
Till with the vision glorious
Her longing eyes are blest,
And the great church victorious
Shall be the church at rest.[6]

18

Sharing in Christ's Sufferings

Please read 1 Peter 4:12–19

Do not be surprised, but rejoice (4:12–14)

No one wants to suffer. When suffering comes to us for following Christ, we are surprised, even shocked and dismayed, especially when our lives have been comfortable. How could our communities or families consider us in the wrong? Why would they mistreat us?

In chapter 4:12 and following, Peter speaks with great tenderness: 'Beloved, do not be surprised at the fiery trial when it comes upon you, as though something strange were happening to you' (4:12). The tone is loving, gentle, and firm at the same time. Persecution, for some including literal fiery trial—Nero was emperor—was coming upon the church. But the fiery trial itself is not the problem Peter addresses. The problem he points out is a response of startled astonishment and fear (cf. 3:14). As a new wave of persecution was about to break on the churches of Asia Minor, the Lord steadies his church using Peter, who had himself both struggled (Luke 22) and triumphed (Acts 5:29) under the pressures of persecution. He reminds us that this should be our expectation in the present world.

Rather than be surprised by persecution and think it strange, the church is 'to rejoice insofar as you share Christ's sufferings, that you may also rejoice and be glad when his glory is revealed' (4:13). Peter is well aware of Jesus' teaching in the sermon on the Mount: "Blessed are those who are persecuted for righteousness' sake ... Rejoice and be glad, for your reward is great in heaven, for so they persecuted the prophets who were before you" (Matthew 5:10–12). Through Peter, our Lord reminds us that where we share in his humiliation, we can expect to share in his exaltation.[1] The day of his return will be a day of exuberant joy for his people.

Peter encourages us further: 'if you are insulted for Christ's name, you are blessed, because the Spirit of glory and of God rests upon you' (4:14). What the world hates is the sight of Christ in us: "because you are not of the world, but I chose you out of the world, therefore the world hates you ... if they persecuted me, they will also persecute you" (John 15:19–20). Where the church or an individual believer suffers for the cause of Christ, it is clear evidence of their union with him. Suffering mistreatment because of Christian faithfulness confirms a great reality: "the Spirit of glory and of God rests upon you" (4:14). Peter draws on the language of Isaiah 11:2, with its prophecy of Spirit of the Lord resting upon the coming Savior. It also echoes Jesus' promise to his disciples of the presence of the Holy Spirit with them (cf. Matthew 10:20; Luke 12:12; John 15:16–17). The comfort is profound: the Triune God is for and with his suffering children (Romans 8:31).

Suffering for Christ, not because of sin (4:15–16)

The rich comfort of this passage of God's Word brings with

it caution and a call to self-examination. Peter has already reminded the church that they can rejoice in suffering, "insofar as you share Christ's sufferings" (4:13) and "if you are insulted for the name of Christ" (4:14). There are sufferings that, though Christians bear them patiently, are not the result of praiseworthy causes. Peter exhorts 'but let none of you suffer as a murderer or a thief or an evildoer or as a meddler' (4:15). Suffering for Christ's sake must not be confused with suffering as a consequence of our own sin, as becomes evident in the subsequent sentence.[2] 'Yet if anyone suffers as a Christian, let him not be ashamed, but let him glorify God in that name' (4:16). There is a close parallel to these verses in the previous chapter: "For what credit is it if, when you sin and are beaten for it, you endure? But if when you do good and suffer for it you endure, this is a gracious thing in the sight of God" (3:20–21). Here, though, there is further instruction for the persecuted. While the world seeks to shame the Christian for their non-conformity to its pursuits, we are not to be ashamed of Christ, bearing his name, nor faithfulness to him—even where we suffer for it. To be ashamed is to shrink back from giving God the glory due him.

Entrusting ourselves to God (4:17–19)

Suffering of any kind, and perhaps especially the suffering of persecution raises the question, why? Calvin states that if a comparison is made it may seem that God allows the reprobate to have a fairly easy life, while being severe towards his children.[3] This troubles us, but the Word provides a humbling and good answer, placing suffering for Christ in the context of God's judgement: 'For it is time for judgement to begin at the household of God; and if it begins with us, what will be the outcome for those who do not obey the gospel of God? And "If the righteous is scarcely saved, what will become of the ungodly and the sinner?"' (4:17–18).

God is perfectly holy, just, wise, and good. Whatever suffering we experience in this life, even the "injustice" of persecution, is far less than what we deserve as sinners. Yet, for those in Christ, his judging of his people "the household of God" (4:17) is not condemning, "but the purging, chastening and purifying of the church by the loving hand of God."[4] It is for our sanctification, our present and eternal good. The contrast set before us in the text is that if God is so serious about our holiness that he allows hardships, even fiery trials of persecution, then what will happen to those who remain in sinful rebellion against him until they die? Spurgeon states, "if God puts even the gold into the fire, what is to become of the dross?"[5] A comfortable life in sin is not better than a life of suffering for Christ: the former ends in judgement to never-ending suffering, the latter concludes in eternal joy, blessedness and peace.

This stark contrast brings us to Peter's conclusion: 'Therefore let those who suffer according to God's will entrust their souls to a faithful Creator while doing good' (4:19). Our lives, including our sufferings are in the Father's hands. The Son, as the captain of our salvation, has also suffered, for us (Hebrews 2:9–18). He has led the way, steadily doing good, through suffering, to glory, "entrusting himself to him who judges justly" (2:23). The faithfulness of God, the Creator of the heavens and earth, is sealed in Christ's suffering, death, resurrection, and ascension. He is ever faithful, "for he cannot deny himself" (2 Timothy 2:13). We have every reason for confidence in him as we follow in his steps.

You and the Word

Have you ever suffered as a consequence of faithfulness to Christ? If you never suffer for Christ, why not? Is it because of complacency or compromise? Is it because you love yourself more than you love God, and as a result there is little or nothing of Christ's character in you? When we suffer it is good for us to reflect on the extent to which our sufferings are because of faithfully following Jesus. When we do suffer for his sake, we have every reason to be profoundly thankful, rejoicing now and being glad when his glory is revealed.

The Head that once was crowned with thorns
Is crowned with glory now;
A royal diadem adorns
The mighty Victor's brow.

The Joy of all who dwell above,
The Joy of all below
To whom he manifests his love,
And grants his Name to know.

To them the cross, with all its shame,
With all its grace, is giv'n;
Their name an everlasting name,
Their joy the joy of heav'n.

They suffer with their Lord below,
They reign with him above;
Their profit and their joy to know
The myst'ry of his love.[6]

19

Shepherd the Flock

Please read 1 Peter 5:1–5

How to Shepherd (5:1–3)

Through his early years as a disciple of Jesus, Peter was characterized by a rough and ready spirit—he was rarely gentle! Yet, in Acts and particularly in Peter's epistles, we see a change: "Peter was not always [this] gentle, but the Spirit of God had rested upon him and now he writes with much tenderness."[1] Peter knows the humility and gentleness of his Lord firsthand. (John 21:15–19)

As an apostle, Peter is in a position of significant leadership and responsibility. Yet he is clearly aware that this does not place him above those to whom he is writing. His words 'so I exhort the elders among you, as a fellow elder' (5:1) personally illustrate God's institution not only of the office of elder, but also the equality in authority that he gives to ordained ministers and elders: they are all fellow elders. The connectedness of the New Testament church is also revealed here. Just as in the Jerusalem council (Acts 15) there is an ongoing connectional ministry of mutual exhortation, encouragement, accountability between the elders of churches, so there is between the churches themselves.

Peter exhorts as a fellow elder 'and a witness of the sufferings of Christ, as well as a partaker in the glory that is going to be revealed' (5:1). He knew Christ's sufferings firsthand; he knew firsthand of his death. Having been Jesus's disciple, Peter is now his apostolic witness. There is also a secondary sense in which Peter is a witness, through the fact that he testified publicly to Christ's sufferings and endured suffering as a result (Acts 2:14–41). It is in and through the Lord Jesus Christ, whom Peter knows (Acts 4:13) and has made known, that Peter shares in the glory which will be made evident to all. The elders and churches of Asia Minor also share in making Christ known and the glory that is going to be revealed. Peter's personal example of shared faith and shared ministry reflects the character of the eldership to which he is called and to which he exhorts them.

The elders are given particular instruction as to their calling: 'shepherd the flock of God that is among you, exercising oversight' (5:2). This call to shepherd includes both feeding and overseeing. Some earlier English translators chose the words, "feed the flock," rather than, "shepherd the flock."[2] While the latter is a more holistically accurate translation, the translators who chose "feed the flock" probably did so thinking of the context of Peter's meeting with Jesus after his resurrection. Three times Jesus asked Peter, "do you love me?" while calling him to "feed my lambs" and "tend my sheep" (John 21:15–17). A key responsibility of elders is to ensure that the church receives spiritual nourishment through faithful preaching of the Word, as well as through private reading and study. Another key responsibility is to "exercise oversight" (5:2), to watch over the flock. Elders are to guard against false shepherding and teaching, keeping each other accountable (cf. Galatians 2:11–16; Titus 1).

They are to warn and discipline sheep who are going astray, comfort and encourage the weak, nurture each one towards greater spiritual vitality, and help members maintain good relations with each other. They cannot do this if they do not know the sheep. They cannot do this if they do not have the heart and mind of Christ.

The following verses give us three parallel sets of practical guidelines to direct elders in serving Christ and his flock with love, preventing abusive ministries. First, elders are to shepherd and exercise oversight 'not under compulsion, but willingly' (5:2). A man ought not serve as an elder in a lazy or minimalist way, needing continual prodding to fulfill his calling. God is glorified when we serve him with willing hearts, actively pursuing what he has called us to.

Second, they are not to serve for 'shameful gain, but eagerly' (5:2). The motivation in serving as an elder must not be financial, social, or other self-gain. The minister who is in love with himself and his ministry, rather than Christ and Christ's ministry, will evidence this in a lack of Christ-like care for the flock. Rather than lovingly laying down his life for the flock, such a minister will expect the flock to lay down their lives for him, wanting money, prestige, or something other than spiritual fruit. God desires his servants to work for the blessing of his people as he does: with joy, with desire, because this is what we want to do as followers of Christ!

Third, elders are to shepherd and exercise oversight, 'not domineering over those in your charge, but being examples to the flock' (5:3). These verses echo the language of Ezekiel 33: "the weak you have not healed, the injured you have not bound up, the strayed you have not brought back, the lost you have not sought, and with force and harshness you have ruled them" (Ezekiel 33:4). Rather than seeking personal dominance over the flock and driving them in convenient directions, ministers and elders are to humbly and diligently lead by example, drawing the flock to follow Christ with them.

The Chief Shepherd's Reward (5:4)

Sometimes Protestants have the mistaken notion that because salvation is by grace alone, through faith alone, in Christ alone, this means that God will not specifically reward his people according to the degree of love, faithfulness, and fruitfulness they showed him in this life. But Scripture often speaks of rewards (cf. Matthew 25:14–30; 1 Corinthians 3:8; 1 Timothy 5:17). Peter brings a similar encouragement to the elders who faithfully pursue their calling from Christ: 'when the chief Shepherd appears, you will receive a crown of glory' (5:4). Our Lord and Savior is the Good Shepherd, the chief shepherd, the shepherd of all of his flock, including the elders he calls to serve. This is why some refer to ministers and elders as "under-shepherds." It is marvelous that the One to whom all praise and honor is due, who works in us to will and to do his good pleasure (Philippians 2:13), will reward and honor his servants for work done by his grace.

The Flock's Responsibility (5:5)

Peter explains the elders' responsibilities not only to the elders, but to the whole church. This is because elders bear accountability not only to each another, but also to the body of Christ (1 Timothy 5:19–20). Peter addresses the congregation's responsibilities, beginning by speaking to young men. 'Likewise, you who are younger, be subject to the elders' (5:5). The young often have the tendency to think themselves knowledgeable and can be headstrong and impetuous—as Peter was as a young disciple. Just as he and the other disciples needed to learn submission to Christ and his kingdom order (cf. Matthew 20:20–28), so do we as church members. We are to submit to the elders' teaching and shepherding as they serve Christ according to his Word (cf. Hebrews 13:7). The word "likewise" (5:5) connects this imperative with the pattern expressed throughout this epistle: citizens are called to submit to governments, servants to masters, wives to husbands, and elders to one another, just as Christ submitted himself to the Father for our salvation (cf. Luke 22:42; Philippians 2:5–8; 1 Peter 2:21, 3:18, 4:1). When we are called to leadership, we are to lead like our Lord Jesus Christ; so also, when we are called to submission, we are to submit like him.

Christ-like submission can only exist where there is humility. We become humble when we become aware of the reality of our own sinfulness and God's undeserved goodness towards us in Christ. We become humble when we come to know Christ and his humility for us. When we live in him, he brings grace to our relationships; we begin to love as he loved us. This is what Peter has in mind as he calls the whole church, ministers and elders included, to 'clothe yourselves, all of you, with humility to each other, for "God opposes the proud but gives grace to the humble"' (5:5). Pride opposes God and God opposes pride. Spurgeon comments, "God has assistance for the humble, but resistance for the proud. Wherever God sees pride lifting itself on high, he resolves to level it in the dust."[3] In contrast to pride, the beautiful humility of Christ brings blessing to us and his whole church.

You and the Word

Self-examination and prayer are indispensable in applying the teaching of God's Word. Pray for his help so that you can repent of remaining sin, receive his forgiveness, grace and strength, and grow in the calling he has given you. Ask yourself what the fruit of your life in the church reveals about the current state of your heart and character before God and his people? Are you proud in yourself or growing in humility in Christ? Do you live as one who is self-sufficient or are you finding your sufficiency in Christ? Do you live with Christ-like submission to the leadership he has ordained in the church, in all that is according to his Word? Do you live with humility towards fellow Christians?

If you are a minister or elder, how can you grow in the way you live out your calling from God? In what ways are you a willing, eager servant of Christ to his people? Do you tend to lead by dominance, social maneuvering, and manipulation, or by the wisdom of the Word and the attraction of a Christ-like example? Do you pursue accountability in your calling, both from your fellow elders and the congregation as a whole? Do you see fellow believers as God's gift to help you grow in serving Christ where you are weak or even failing in your calling? Ask your heavenly Father to conform you more and more to Christ.

Take my life and let it be,
Consecrated, Lord, to thee.
Take my moments, and my days,
Let them flow in endless praise.[4]

20

The Perseverance of the Church

Please read 1 Peter 5:6–14

Humility in Suffering (5:6–7)

When suffering comes into our lives it always comes within God's will and purpose. It is never arbitrary; it is never meaningless. Our Lord is "righteous in all his ways, and kind in all his works" (Psalm 145:17). While there are varied reasons for suffering, some of which we may never know in this life (Luke 13:1–5; cf. Job), there is one response to suffering which Scripture repeatedly presents as God glorifying: humility.

The wider context to verse 6 is in the latter part of chapter four, where Peter calls the church not to be surprised at the fiery trial that is coming upon them. They are to be aware that God's judgement begins with his church (cf. Hebrews 12:3–11), humbly entrust themselves to him, and continue doing good. Our God-given sufferings are designed for us with a God-given end in view: 'humble yourselves, therefore under the mighty hand of

God, so that at the proper time he may exalt you' (5:6). This "light momentary affliction is preparing for us an eternal weight of glory beyond all comparison" (2 Corinthians 4:17).

The more we understand these things, the more we will see that it is good and fitting to humble ourselves by 'casting all your anxieties on him, because he cares for you' (5:7). Pride clings to anxieties, as though worrying will bring better resolution than the Lord will when we give our cares to him. As Hebrews 12 reminds us, God's mighty hand is a loving fatherly hand for his children. We have every reason to give him our burdens and rest. Matthew Henry reminds us that, "He is willing to release you of your care, and take the care of you upon himself. He will either avert what you fear, or support you under it."[1]

Resisting Satan (5:8–9)

Humbly resting in Christ through trials does not imply a complacent Christian life. As we pursue resting more fully in him, we are also called to 'be sober-minded; be watchful. Your adversary the devil prowls around like a roaring lion, seeking someone to devour' (5:8). The illustration Peter uses is particularly vivid for those who have lived in rural parts of Africa and India, with the roar of prowling lions echoing through the night. Living in this context requires clear-headed, careful awareness of one's surroundings.

Satan's threats and assaults manifest in a variety of ways. In the West, with its rampant idolatry and distortion of sexuality, there is the roar of social revolutionaries pursuing legislation, lawsuits, and fines against those who will not join with them in reframing society. The temptations include acquiescing through fear and being enticed to sins that are an offense to God and destructive to individuals, families and churches. In other regions there are societal and cultural pressures on Christians from dominant Islamism, Hinduism, Buddhism, secular dictatorships, or endemic corruption and crime. Around the world pornography and an open invitation to immorality is present 24/7 online. Just as the devil's temptations come in many forms, so do his threats. We need the sober-mindedness and watchfulness that comes from close communion with God to accurately discern the spiritual dangers of our own contexts. Minds clouded by self-absorption, entertainment, or busyness that preoccupies will be weak and prone to capitulation.

In response to the assaults of Satan we are called to 'resist him, firm in your faith, knowing that the same kinds of suffering are being experienced by your brotherhood throughout the world' (5:9). We resist Satan by holding fast to the Word of God (cf. Ephesians 6:10–20; 1 John 5:1–5). There is great comfort here: the spiritual opposition we face is not new, nor are we at any time alone in facing such trials (cf. Acts 7:51–53; Hebrews 2:14–18). Many have walked this road before us, many are now walking it with us. Growing awareness of the global church is one way we can bring further application of this encouragement to ourselves and others. Peter's reminder is Hebrews': take courage, you are "surrounded by a great cloud of witnesses" (Hebrews 12:1).

God's Work in You (5:10–11)

Verse 10 wonderfully reaffirms God's purpose and control in our sufferings: 'and after you have suffered a little while, the God of all grace, who has called you to his eternal glory in Christ, will himself restore, confirm, strengthen, and establish you' (5:10). When and what we will suffer is not primary; how we bear, respond to, and grow through suffering is. Our sufferings not only test the genuineness of our faith, but are also instruments for our sanctification. God selects and uses them with perfect wisdom and intention for us. He is the God of all grace. Peter reminds us that this God is the one "who has called you to his eternal glory in Christ" (5:10), the one who has pursued us by his

Word and Spirit for salvation through his Son. He will restore every loss we suffer. He will fulfill every promise. If God is for us, who can stand against us?

Filled with this encouragement from the Holy Spirit, Peter begins praising: 'To him be the dominion forever and ever. Amen' (5:11). Our Triune God is worthy of eternal dominion and has eternal dominion for he is God, and God alone. He is exalted forever. We have every reason to rest and rejoice in him, while those attempting rebellion against him have every reason to tremble: "Blessed are all who take refuge in him" (Psalm 2:12).

Greetings and the Peace of Christ (5:12–14)

The remaining verses are the postscript of the epistle. Peter writes with the help 'of Silvanus, a faithful brother as I regard him' (5:12). Silvanus may have served as scribe to Peter, but was more likely the ministerial bearer of the letter to the churches, and would have read and then explained and applied it to them (cf. 2 Corinthians 1:19). He served in ministry with Peter, and also Paul and Timothy. Peter commends him as trustworthy so that those who first received the letter would have confidence that Silvanus is bringing God's Word to them.

Peter adds that he has only written briefly in this epistle, but, 'exhorting and declaring that this is the true grace of God. Stand firm in it' (5:12). Peter's love for Christ and his sheep is evident. His words indicate his desire to communicate more to them, his passion is that we live in God's grace. Once more, his exhortation is to hold fast to what is true. Jesus has enabled Peter to love him, and feed and tend his sheep.

As in many of the epistles, our Lord includes personal greetings to the congregation. The connections between individuals and congregations that make one, mutually accountable church, is not merely a matter of organization. It is the vital, organic reality of the body of Christ, his bride

(Ephesians 4:4–6). Peter shares with the congregations of Asia Minor that, 'she who is at Babylon, who is likewise chosen, sends you greetings, as does Mark my son' (5:13). Translators have wrestled over who this refers to. Is it an individual, perhaps Peter's wife? Earlier English translators believed that Peter was giving the greetings of a congregation in Mesopotamia, where he labored.[2] Others have argued that it does signify a congregation, but note that there were a number of places named Babylon at this point, even in Egypt. Still others say that it is an allegorical reference to Rome. "Mark my son" may refer to Peter's biological son, particularly if he previously refers to his wife. Or it may be John Mark, who accompanied Paul in his ministry and, according to early church history, wrote the gospel of Mark with Peter's help. While the exact answer is uncertain, what is clear is that Peter communicates Christ's love to the congregations of Asia Minor from fellow Christians. Peter indicates that in the church, love and concern for congregations beyond our own are to be made evident.

When Peter says, 'Greet one another with the kiss of love' (5:14), some of us are uncomfortable. But in the near East and Mediterranean kissing was and remains a customary form of greeting among family members and close friends, displaying warmth and affection. Fellow-believers were to be greeted with similar affection (cf. Luke 15:20; Acts 20:37), as siblings in Christ—family whom we gladly welcome.

Peter's final words are a benediction for believers and their children living by faith: 'Peace to all of you who are in Christ' (5:13). The benediction reminds those not yet in Christ, that outside of him there is no blessing, no peace. For those in Christ, it is a rich assurance that Jesus has reconciled them to God.

You and the Word

The great themes of this epistle, hope in Christ and pursuit of holiness, are brought to conclusion in the final verses. Our sin, sufferings, and Satan's attacks are no match for our Savior. He is worthy of our complete confidence and thankful pursuit of continued growth in grace. He will restore, confirm, strengthen and establish his people (5:10). He is worthy of our praise:

> Oh, the depth of the riches of the wisdom and knowledge of God!
> How unsearchable are his judgements and how inscrutable his ways!
> For from him and through him and to him are all things.
> To him be glory forever. Amen. (Romans 11:33, 36)

The Second Epistle of Peter: Truth and Triumph (2 Peter 1–3)

1

The God Who Gives

Please read 2 Peter 1:1–4

The Writer and Hearers (1:1–2)

The same Peter writes this second epistle: the man named Simon, called from fishing by our Lord and given the new name "Peter" (cf. Luke 5:1–11, 6:13–14). Written near the end of his life (c.AD 64–67), Peter's second epistle displays the same humility of spirit in his first epistle. God's gracious, continued work in Peter is evident. By the Holy Spirit's leading he introduces his apostolic authorship with the memory of his own transformation: 'Simon Peter, a servant and apostle of Jesus Christ' (1:1). The Greek word translated into the English here as "servant," commonly referred to servants who were bought at a price as "bond-servants" or slaves.[1] They were not independent, but belonged in the whole of their being to their master, living under his ownership and authority. Peter is stating that he is a man whom Christ purchased, subject to and serving him. At the same time, he is an apostle, a term first used in the gospels at Jesus' appointment of the twelve (cf. Mark 3:14). The apostles were Christ's messengers, placed in a unique calling in the early church to lead and instruct, and at times inspired to write epistles or books as part of the New Testament canon. Peter is called by Jesus and bears his message.

As we read this epistle it is clear that it was also first addressed to the same congregations of Asia Minor as the first epistle: "this is now the second letter that I am writing to you, beloved" (3:1). At the same time, the apostle writes with the awareness that this was God's Word for the entire church, including the future church—all 'those who have obtained a faith of equal standing with ours by the righteousness of our God and Savior Jesus Christ' (1:1).

The Christians of Asia Minor shared the same faith with the apostles—a faith equally precious and valuable to them all. The order of the sentence highlights an important truth: while we are justified by faith alone, Peter reminds us that our faith itself is the gift of God, received from him. He has given us faith in his righteousness. Faith is worked in us by the Holy Spirit, sent through the faithfulness of the Father (John 14:16), who promised his Son a willing people (Psalm 110:3) clothed in his righteousness. This epistle is written to those who live by this faith from God.

The opening concludes with a blessing: 'May grace and peace be multiplied to you in the knowledge of God and of Jesus our Lord' (1:2). Peter wants the church to experience more and more of God's grace, and saving and sanctifying love, along with the comfort and assurance that they are his. Peace comes with the knowledge that we are fully reconciled to God through Christ, adopted as his children, tenderly cared for and protected in all things. Peter emphasizes that the blessings of grace and peace are increased by "the knowledge of God and Jesus our Lord" (1:2). It is knowledge of God that opens richest blessing. We are humbled, our minds are expanded, and our hearts challenged and encouraged as we grow in this.

God's Provision and Purpose (1:3–4)

God provides for all of our needs in Christ. 'His divine power has granted to us all things that pertain to life and godliness' (1:3). Giving people "all that pertains to life and godliness" is God's gracious, powerful work. Alexander Nisbet states: "To give grace to a graceless soul is a work of God's infinite power, there being so much unworthiness, guiltiness, and opposition to hinder that work in all the elect ... the Lord works irresistibly and freely."[2] Satan's schemes and our sinful hearts are no match for God's power. Because God is holy and good, the exercise of his power is always holy and good. In perfect awareness of our hopeless situation, he provides everything we need. While Peter is certainly aware that the Lord provides for and sustains our earthly lives, his focus here is on the new, eternal life and godliness, given to the elect in Christ—from regeneration and justification to sanctification and glorification. All of this is granted to us, signed and sealed to us in Jesus' blood.

The way that God brings us into this vast blessing in Christ is by making himself known to us by his Word: 'through the knowledge of him who called us to his own glory and excellence' (1:3).[3] In Hebrews we read that God spoke long ago at many times and in many ways to our fathers, "but in these last days he has spoken to us by his Son" who is "the radiance of the glory of God and the exact imprint of his nature" (Hebrews 1:1–3). In his high priestly prayer, Jesus said, "this is eternal life, that they know you the only true God, and Jesus Christ whom you have sent ... I have given them the words that you gave me" (John 17:3, 8). As we come to know the Triune God, through the Son, we see his glory and excellence, and marvel that he has called us to himself.

As we come to know Christ, through whom we receive all things, we also realize that God 'has granted to us his precious and very great promises' (1:4). God's word is full of rich promises, from the promise of a Savior in Genesis 3 to the promise of the coming end to evil and a new created order in Revelation. God's faithfulness to us in Christ, expressed in his promises, is 'so that through them you may become partakers of the divine nature' (1:4).

The apostle chose his words carefully. Partaking in the divine nature means being conformed to the character of God, not participating in his being.[4] For those who receive God's promises by faith, even as they are given the grace of faith, the Lord begins to transform them to be more like him. The Christian begins to grow, "to resemble him in heavenly wisdom, holiness, uprightness, and other of his communicable properties, especially in humility, self-denial, love and pity toward other miserable sinners, zeal for the Lord's honour, and such as other perfections as were eminent in the Man Christ."[5]

The change that takes place as a sinner is saved by the divine power of God, and set apart to a new, growing life of holiness in communion with God, reflects another profound reality. Not only have we become partakers in the divine nature, we have also 'escaped from the corruption that is in the world because of sinful desire' (1:4). An amazing deliverance has taken place. We were once spiritually dead in our sins. We were walking in the ways of a fallen world, following Satan's lead, pursuing our own passions as children of wrath. God, in his rich mercy, because of his great love, provided escape. By his divine power he has given everything for our salvation in Christ. "Amazing love, how can it be?"[6]

You and the Word

Grace and peace are multiplied to us as we grow in knowing and communing with God and Jesus our Lord (1:2). In a sermon on the blessedness of knowing God, Spurgeon says:

> The proper study of God's elect is God; the proper study of

a Christian is the Godhead. The highest science, the loftiest speculation, the mightiest philosophy, which can ever engage the attention of a child of God, is the name, the nature, the person, the work, the doings, and the existence of the great God whom he calls his Father. There is something exceedingly improving to the mind in a contemplation of the Divinity. It is a subject so vast, that all our thoughts are lost in its immensity; so deep, that our pride is drowned in its infinity ... No subject of contemplation will tend more to humble the mind, than thoughts of God. We shall be obliged to feel—

"Great God, how infinite art thou,
What worthless worms are we!"

But while the subject *humbles* the mind it also *expands* it. Nothing will so enlarge the intellect, nothing so magnify the whole soul of man, as a devout, earnest, continued investigation of the great subject of the Deity. And, whilst humbling and expanding, this subject is eminently *consolatory*. Oh, there is, in contemplating Christ, a balm for every wound; in musing on the Father, there is a quietus for every grief; and in the influence of the Holy Ghost, there is a balsam for every sore. Would you lose your sorrows? Would you drown your cares? Then go, plunge yourself in the Godhead's deepest sea; be lost in his immensity; and you shall come forth as from a couch of rest, refreshed and invigorated.[7]

2

A Useful, Fruitful Life

Please read 2 Peter 1:5–15

Motivation for Sanctification (1:5)

Having opened our eyes to God's provision of escape from death (1:1–4), Peter tells us 'for this very reason make every effort to supplement,' or add to, 'your faith' (1:5). God's salvation is not merely to forgive us, essential as that is. It is also the beginning of a growing new life in fellowship with him. His gracious and powerful deliverance of his children does not lead to complacency or contentment with remaining sin. Those who claim to be Christ's but say "I am who I am, don't expect me to change much; God loves me just the way I am," show a spirit incompatible with Christ's person and work. Those who are his hunger and thirst for righteousness; they realize that in belonging to him they are incompatible with the sin that has shaped their character (Matthew 5:6). They realize that the Lord Jesus gave himself for them, and that he is all-sufficient for sanctification. We have every reason to pursue multi-faceted growth with humble diligence and determination, in love for him. God's children desire personal godliness and they are to work hard at it.

Seven Qualities (1:5–7)

The call to add to our faith is a call to active pursuit of Christward change in our hearts, minds, and actions. The holistic nature of the character transformation becomes clear as Peter directs us to a list of seven qualities similar to those found in Galatians 5:22–23. His literary form in listing these fruits with repetition, indicates an ongoing, hard-working cultivation. 'Make every effort to supplement your faith with virtue, and virtue with knowledge, and knowledge with self-control, and self-control with steadfastness, and steadfastness with godliness, and godliness with brotherly affection, and brotherly affection with love' (1:5–7). There is no room for passivity here.

What exactly is in view in each of these qualities? The list begins with the word translated as 'virtue'; other English possibilities are moral excellence, or goodness (1:5). Calvin comments, "I take virtue to mean a life honest and rightly formed ... moral goodness."[1] Pictured here is the pursuit of a life of ethical excellence, summed up by the Ten Commandments (Exodus 20:1–17), and expounded by Jesus in the Sermon on the Mount (Matthew 5–7). In faith in Christ and gratitude to God, the man or woman who is passionate about the pursuit of virtue delights in God's law and studies it for personal growth: "Oh how I love your law! It is my meditation all the day" (Psalm 119:97; Psalm 19:7–10).

'Knowledge' (1:5–6) is to be added to our faith as well. Peter has already used a similar term twice in the epistle, in reference to knowing "God and Jesus our Lord" (1:2–3). Having the degree of understanding of our Lord and Savior that we do should draw us to pursue a far greater and more accurate knowledge of our Triune God. For Christians, knowing and loving God are inseparably connected (1 John 4:7–19). Adding knowledge to our faith also means pursuing growth in a right understanding of creation, especially of ourselves and those around us. We need to grow in a right understanding of this present world: seeing sin and corruption for what they really are. We must be "transformed by the renewal of your mind, that by testing you may discern what is the will of God, what is good and acceptable and perfect" (Romans 12:2).

'Self-control' (1:6)—"temperance" or "self-discipline"—is next on Peter's list. The false teachers Peter warns against later lack self-control; they are slaves of their passions and corruption (2:2, 10, 14, 18–19). Nisbet states, "a Christian that would grow must labor to have, by the power of God's grace in him, such a command over his passions of anger, fear ... and especially in the use of sensual delights, that he may be able to keep them within the bounds which ... the rules of God's word prescribes."[2] Growing in self-control preserves us from many sins against God and our neighbors, enabling us to harness our passions for good.

'Steadfastness' (1:6), like the other qualities Peter gives, coheres seamlessly with this. As we live by faith, pursuing moral excellence, knowledge, and self-control in Christ, we will also be able to pursue growth in steadfastness. An increasingly steadfast man or woman finds they are not as easily shaken or moved off course by temptations or afflictions as they once were. Growth in endurance through trials and perseverance in what is holy and good, is growth in Christ-likeness. "Consider him who endured" (Hebrews 12:3); his grace is sufficient for you to intentionally pursue greater steadfastness to his glory.

'Godliness' (1:6–7) is a quality which is very close to and overlaps with holiness. Holiness refers to being set apart to God; godliness emphasizes devotion to God from another vantage. It refers to a God-ward heart attitude and direction which impacts our actions. As a heart attitude towards God, godliness is comprised of three elements: "the fear of God, the love of God, and the desire for God."[3] The apostle Paul, warning against "different doctrine" which "does not agree with the sound words of our Lord Jesus Christ," calls us to be devoted to, "teaching that accords with godliness," adding the encouragement that, "there is great gain in godliness with contentment" (1 Timothy 6:3–6). This is the godliness in which Peter wants us to grow.

While the primary focus of godliness is God-ward, 'brotherly affection' (1:7) is a fruit of faith directed towards those around us. Lenski reflects, "the godly must cling together like so many brothers of one family, like so many friends, in close friendship and friendliness."[4] Peter's first epistle views the same fruit rising out of new life in Christ: "having purified your souls by your obedience to the truth for a sincere brotherly love, love one another earnestly from a pure heart" (1 Peter 1:21). Fellow Christians are to be viewed and cared for as brothers and sisters, family in the Lord.

The final quality our Lord calls us to add to our faith in this list is 'love' (1:7). Scripture frequently commends love as one of the primary fruits of the Spirit (cf. 1 Corinthians 13; 2 Corinthians 6:6; Galatians 5:22; Ephesians 4:2; 1 Timothy 4:12; Revelation 2:19). Like the other qualities, the source of love is found in God himself: "God so loved the world, that he gave his only begotten Son, that whoever believes in him should not perish, but have eternal life" (John 3:16). The apostle John later reminds us that, "by this we know love, that he laid down his life for us, and we ought to lay down our lives for the brothers," loving in "deed and truth" (1 John 3:16–18). God's love is made manifest to us in Christ. When it transforms us, we make that love manifest to those around us. Peter knew this experience well (John 21:15–17).

Sanctification versus stagnation (1:8–11)

The imperative of pursuing spiritual growth in these areas is reinforced with the promise in verse 8 that 'if these qualities are yours and are increasing, they keep you from being ineffective or unfruitful in the knowledge of the Lord Jesus Christ' (1:8). Calvin reflects, "the knowledge of Christ is an efficacious thing and a living root, which brings forth fruit."[5] Where the qualities of virtue, knowledge, self-control, steadfastness, godliness, brotherly affection, and love are cultivated, we become increasingly useful and fruitful in serving our Lord and Savior.

Peter strongly emphasizes a negative contrast in the next verse: 'For whoever lacks these qualities is so nearsighted that he is blind, having forgotten that he was cleansed from his former sins' (1:9). We are saved by faith alone, by grace alone, through Christ alone. Yet, true faith is never *alone*; it always bears the fruit of these qualities to some increasing extent. "Faith by itself, if it does not have works, is dead" (James 2:17). A stagnant Christian life, lacking growth in the fruits of faith, is at best a life on a backsliding trajectory. Though such an individual may still intellectually understand the gospel, they are in danger of losing a heart understanding of who Christ is, and what he has done to forgive their sins. They have been blinded.

With this warning in mind, our Lord, urges and encourages us onward. 'Therefore, brothers, be all the more diligent to confirm your calling and election, for if you practice these qualities you will never fall' (1:10). There is an alternative to falling away from Christ: it is found in the practice of holiness. In fact, diligent pursuit of the qualities listed in this passage actually serves to confirm our calling and election. As we seek to grow, looking to Jesus's grace, our faith itself is confirmed and our assurance grows. Why? Because Christ's faithfulness and sufficiency is increasingly realized in and by us. He is the one who perfectly lived all of these qualities in our place, bearing our guilt and penalty for living the very opposite of these qualities in sin. As we come to and live in him, Jesus forgives our sin, cleanses us, and gives us all we need to grow in each of these qualities.

The diligent pursuit of growth in the fruits of faith anticipates a glorious future. 'For in this way there will be richly provided for you an entrance into the eternal kingdom of our Lord and Savior Jesus Christ' (1:11). Some Christians' works will be burned up and they will suffer loss, "though he himself will be saved, but only as through fire" (1 Corinthians 3:15). This is not the case for those who pursue Christ's call with diligence. They will enter heavenly glory and the new heavens and earth hearing the words, "well done, good and faithful servant ... enter into the joy of your master" (Matthew 25:23).

Needed Reminders (1:12–15)

Peter is well aware of the need for believers to be reminded of the upward calling of life in Christ. 'Therefore', he says, 'I intend always to remind you of these qualities, though you know them and are established in the truth that you have' (1:12). We tend to forget. The sin that remains in us as Christians tries to pull us to inertia and decline. Peter's awareness of our ongoing spiritual needs serves to remind us of what we have been saved for—a life overflowing with glorifying and enjoying God. This is what pastors do: Peter's remindings demonstrate a faithful ministry in Christ. "If ministers be negligent in their work," says Matthew Henry, "it can hardly be expected that the people will be diligent in theirs; therefore Peter will not be negligent, but ... diligent" in reminding the church of God's promises and precepts.[6]

The urgency of Peter's calling is only heightened by the awareness of the limited time of ministry he still has. 'I think it right, as long as I am in this body, to stir you up by way of reminder, since I know that the putting off of my body will be soon, as our Lord Jesus Christ has made clear to me' (1:13–14). He feels like his time on earth is running out. The apostle provides a pattern for us. He knows that the day Jesus spoke about with him is coming soon (John 21:18–19). The awareness of our own limited days in this present life should impel us to use them well. This includes stirring each other up to more full and fruitful life in Christ, "encouraging one another, and all the more as you see the Day drawing near" (Hebrews 10:25)

Peter's final words in this section find fulfillment in their distribution: his putting them in print, and form a transition into what follows: 'And I will make every effort so that after my departure you may be able at any time to recall these things' (1:15). Though he is dead, he still speaks (Hebrews 11:4). The Lord Jesus Christ saved Peter, and he was the One sanctifying Peter by his Word and Spirit, through his apostolic ministry. At the same time Peter not only lived by faith in Christ, but was called by him to expend effort, as recorded here. The incredible result is that Peter, by the inspiration of the Holy Spirit, penned two epistles that enable the church to recall these things at any time, to the day of Christ's return.

You and the Word

God's call is to active, passionate pursuit of sanctification in Christ Jesus his Son. The way to be stirred up and renewed in this is by being reminded and refreshed in who he is, what he has done for us, is doing for us, and is calling us to. The means he has given for us are simple enough for a child and deeper than the most mature Christian: engagement in public worshiping; reading his Word; prayer; receiving the sacraments; and being part of the communion of his people. Together these create the environment for healthy spiritual growth and great fruitfulness.

> Create in me a clean heart, O God,
> and renew a right spirit within me ...

Restore to me the joy of your salvation,
And uphold me with a willing spirit. (Psalm 51:10–12)

Peter's Last
Will & Testament

3

Why We Obey the Word

Please read 2 Peter 1:16–21

Eyewitnesses of the majesty of Jesus Christ (1:16–18)

Peter has just declared his commitment to always be ready to remind the church of God's calling to us in Christ (1:12–15), Well aware of the false teachers who will echo Satan's ancient lie—"has God really said?"—he now explains why we should hear and obey God's Word. False teachers challenged not only the apostles' ministry, but also their message. Peter states: 'for we did not follow cleverly devised myths when we made known the power and coming of our Lord Jesus Christ, but we were eyewitnesses of his glory' (1:16). The claim that the apostolic proclamation of Christ was a clever myth was a direct attack on Christ's person and work, and thus on the church. No doubt Peter remembered well the parable of Jesus regarding the sowing of the seed. He was well aware that Satan would try every means to snatch away, distract from, or choke out the life giving Word (Matthew 13:1–23).

Peter and the other apostles were eyewitnesses of the majesty of the Lord Jesus Christ. They were with him in his earthly ministry, witnessed his death, resurrection, and ascension to heavenly glory (1 Corinthians 15:1–8). The apostles saw, heard, felt, tangibly experienced the Lord's coming and power. In verse 16, Peter

> distinctly mentions two things, that Christ had been manifested in the flesh, and also that power was manifested by him. Thus, then, we have the whole gospel; for we know that he, the long-promised Redeemer, came from heaven, put on our flesh, lived in the world, died, and rose again; and, in the second place, we perceive the end and fruit of all these things, that is, that he might be God with us ... that he might cleanse us ... and consecrate us ..., that he might deliver us from hell, and raise us up to heaven, that he might by the sacrifice of his death make an atonement for the sins of the world, that he might reconcile us to the Father, that he might become to us the author of righteousness and life.[1]

Directed by the Spirit to remind us that he is an eyewitness, Peter brings us back to the great confirmation of Jesus' person and work at the Mount of Transfiguration. Peter himself heard the Father's voice. 'For when [Jesus] received honor and glory from the Father, and the voice was borne to him by the Majestic Glory, "This is my beloved Son in whom I am well pleased," we ourselves heard this very voice borne from heaven, for we were with him on the holy mountain' (1:17–18; Matthew 17:5–6). God the Father confirms, honors, and glorifies his Son—declaring his delight in the perfect sufficiency of his person and work—in the eye-witness presence of the apostles.

The Word Confirmed (1:19–21)

The experience of being with Jesus on the Mount of Transfiguration, and hearing God the Father speak must have been stunning and formative. But Peter tells us there is something even more sure. God has given us something better than Noah's experience of deliverance through the flood, than Moses parting of the Red Sea, better than the Father's audible voice and the Son's Transfiguration. God's revelation in his inscripturated Word is even more full, extensive, complete, and enduring. 'And we have something more sure, the prophetic word, to which you will do well to pay attention as to a lamp shining in a dark place, until the day dawns and the morning star arises in your hearts' (1:19).

Like Paul (2 Corinthians 4:5–6), Peter draws on language used by the apostle John. The Word illumines the darkness. Christ is "the light [who] shines in the darkness ... the true light, which enlightens everyone" (John 1:5, 9). He is the bright morning star (Revelation 22:16). There is a marvelous unity with Old Testament revelation. Isaiah declared: "Arise, shine, for your light has come, and the glory of the Lord has risen upon you" (Isaiah 60:1). Knowing that the light of the fullness of God's revelation has come to us reminds us of the urgency of paying careful attention to what God says to us (cf. Hebrews 1:1–2, 2:1–4).

Despite the claims by false teachers, the Scriptures are not the musings of private individuals, nor creative writing projects of people from different ages. How did Moses write the Pentateuch? How did scribes and prophets write the other Old Testament books? What about the gospels and epistles comprising the New Testament? The answer Peter says comes by 'knowing this first of all, that no prophecy of Scripture comes from someone's own interpretation. For no prophecy was ever produced by the will of man, but men spoke from God as they were carried along by the Holy Spirit' (1:20–21). God's Word is God's work. The Holy Spirit prompted, gave, and directed the exact content of the Scriptures to the writers, by them producing the canon of the Old and New Testaments. God graciously stooped down, using men, with their characters, abilities, and experiences, speaking through them and by them to us. In doing so, he perfectly and accurately revealed himself to us in ways that we can understand. The result is the complete, authoritative, sufficient, infallible and inerrant Word.

You and the Word

The Word of God is a priceless treasure; it is the revelation of God, in writing, to us. How do you handle the Word? What place does it have in your life? The quality and quantity of attention we give to God's Word and the spirit in which we respond to it may give us reason to tremble. Yet as we consider his Word, we should be filled with wonder: his Word is richly gracious. Our Lord not only exposes and illuminates our sin and the judgment we deserve, but he also reveals the riches of his grace to us in Christ: welcoming us to himself with the free offer of forgiveness, reconciliation and new life. God gives us Jesus, his Son, in the Word, in whom "are hidden all the treasures of wisdom and knowledge." (Colossians 2:3) No wonder the Psalmist sings:

> How sweet are your words to my taste,
> Sweeter than honey to my mouth! ...
> I love your commandments above gold, above fine gold.
> Therefore I consider all your precepts to be right; I hate every false way.
> Your testimonies are wonderful; therefore my soul keeps them.
> The unfolding of your words gives light; it imparts understanding to the simple.
> I open my mouth and pant, because I long for your commandments.
> Turn to me and be gracious to me, as is your way with those who love your name. (Psalm 119:103, 127–132)

False Teachers Among You

Please read 2 Peter 2:1–22

They Will Come (2:1–3)

The inspired Word comes to us through the prophets and apostles of our Lord (1:16–21), yet there are critics of the Word. Peter reminds us that their existence is not a new problem. 'But false prophets also arose among the people, just as there will be false teachers among you' (2:1). The first false prophet, Satan, deceptively distorted the truth in the Garden, asking "did God actually say ...?" (Genesis 3:1) A long line of false prophets ensued. Many of the kings of Israel and Judah surrounded themselves with false prophets who assured peace and prosperity while simultaneously promoting idolatry, corruption and gross wickedness. God declared through Jeremiah, "they heal the brokenness of the daughter of My people superficially, saying, 'Peace, peace', but there is no peace" (Jeremiah 8:10–11).

The false prophets of the Old Testament, like Eli's sons

(1 Samuel 2:12–25), often rose up from within the covenant community. We also must live with the awareness that false teachers will rise among us in the New Testament era; they will come from among those whom we thought were disciples of Jesus (2:1). Taking this warning seriously produces a right vigilance for the gospel of the Lord Jesus Christ. It exposes the tactics of the enemies of Christ and his church, 'who will secretly bring in destructive heresies, even denying the Master who bought them, bringing upon themselves swift destruction' (2:1). Peter describes false teachers as secretive because the shift in their teaching is often subtle. They use familiar Christian terms, but with altered definitions and "mixed with many precious truths."[1] False teachers can come across with great sincerity, whether as young, bright, and zealous or as kindly older men or women. The reason they can speak with apparent utter sincerity is in part because of their blindness (Matthew 15:14). But their teaching is deadly. It ends in a rejection of Christ and his salvation, leaving both the teachers and followers in a desperate condition of "bringing upon themselves swift destruction" (2:1).

Despite their deadly errors, false teachers have little difficulty gaining a following—at least for a time. 'Many will follow their sensuality, and because of them the way of truth will be blasphemed' (2:2). While sometimes the primary attraction to false teaching is pride, often other sins are mixed in, forming an intoxicating combination that gains followers. The word translated in the English Standard Version as "sensuality" and "shameful ways" in the New International Version, "often refers to sexual sin in the New Testament ... the same is likely true here as well."[2] False teaching, whether it tends toward legalism or antinomianism, always gives increased space to sin—a necessary consequence of minimizing the person and work of Christ. The false Christianity of false teachers is blasphemy: it makes a mockery of Jesus Christ by lessening, distorting, or denying his person and work.

While they love "ministry" and a following, false teachers lack genuine love for Christ, and for his flock. 'In their greed they will exploit you with false words. Their condemnation from long ago is not idle, and their destruction is not asleep' (2:3). Rather than loving, sacrificial shepherds, they are manipulative flatterers, hungry for what they can gain from the church. The King James Version puts it well when stating, "they ... make merchandise of you" (2:3) They will quickly cut off those who begin to raise concerns, and abandon those of no use to them. Sheep are a commodity in which false shepherds deal.

But Peter reaffirms the terrifying position that the false teachers are in themselves as they lead men and women away from Christ. Nothing is hidden from God's sight. He has known the false teachers from before the foundation of the earth: they only live and move and have their being because of him. Their rebellion hurries them along to their destruction.

Judgement and Deliverance (4–10a)

In describing the fearful end of false teachers, Peter looks at three case studies from the Old Testament era: fallen angels, the pre-flood world, and Sodom and Gomorrah. He does so using the literary device of one long sentence, creating a rising crescendo of "if" statements, concluding with the "then" in verse 9.

The first "if" statement is: 'For if God did not spare angels when they sinned, but cast them into hell and committed them to chains of gloomy darkness to be kept until the judgment' (2:4). Fallen angels did not escape God's judgement. Peter's next statement indicates not only God's just, awe-inducing judgement, but also his faithful deliverance of his people. Aware of the anxiety that warnings of false teachers can create in believers' hearts, he reminds us that the Lord was faithful to keep Noah in the middle of mocking and catastrophe. 'If he did not spare the ancient world, but preserved Noah, a herald of righteousness, with seven others, when he brought a flood upon the world of the ungodly' (2:5). The pattern of both God's judgement and deliverance is repeated in the following verses. However, Peter now heightens the message by including explicit reference to what is coming in the future. 'If by turning the cities of Sodom and Gomorrah to ashes he condemned them to extinction, making them an example of what is going to happen to the ungodly' (2:6). Matthew Henry reflects, "he who keeps fire and water from hurting his people (Isaiah 43:2), can make either to destroy his enemies ... they are never safe."[3] Judgement of the unrepentant is a means of deliverance for God's children.

In his third case study, Peter gives a more extensive description of God's preservation and deliverance of his people, bringing us to the concluding "then": 'And if he rescued righteous Lot, greatly distressed by the sensual conduct of the wicked (for as the righteous man lived among them day after day, he was tormenting his righteous soul over their lawless deeds that he saw and heard); then the Lord knows how to rescue the godly from trials, and to keep the unrighteous under punishment until the day of judgement, and especially those who indulge in the lust of defiling passion and despise authority' (2:7–10a). Lot lived a righteously troubled life in a context where false teaching and sexual immorality dominated. If God could rescue both Noah and Lot, then he certainly knows how to rescue us from both the temptation of false teachers and the trials and sufferings that they bring to the church. If he cast fallen angels into hell, destroyed the world with the flood, turned Sodom and Gomorrah to ash, then he is certainly able to bring justice to those who rebel against his authority while pretending to be his servants. This solemn message is a great comfort for the child of God.

Rebellion and Consequences (10b–22)

Peter now turns to bring us to see why God is just in dealing severely with false teachers: their defiance, depravity, and deception are "monstrous arrogance" and evil.[4] 'Bold and willful, they do not tremble as they blaspheme the glorious ones, whereas angels, though greater in might and power, do not pronounce a blasphemous judgement against them before the Lord' (2:10b–11). While commentators have wrestled over whether "glorious ones" refers to angels, government officials, or ministers, the latter seems likely in this context. Another possibility is that the term can also be translated "glories" and may refer to the "glories" of Christ directly (1 Peter 1:11).[5] What is very clear is the contrast Peter makes. False teachers revile those whom God has ordained, even Christ himself, while the holy angels, whose power and understanding of wickedness are great, do not bring mocking accusations against the false teachers. 'But these, like irrational animals, creatures of instinct, born to be caught and destroyed, blaspheming about matters of which they are ignorant, will also be destroyed in their destruction, suffering wrong as the wage for their wrongdoing' (2:12–13a). Their arrogance flows from the instinct of evil within. While they have apparent knowledge, they are actually blind towards the very realities they claim to know insightfully. The devastation they cause will envelope and utterly devastate them.

While false teachers are in love with sin, at times even brazenly so, they are adept at living a duplicitous life. 'They count it pleasure to revel in the daytime. They are blots and blemishes, reveling in their deceptions while they feast with you' (2:13). On the one hand they will seek out opportunity for sin, on the other they are fully engaged, even leading apparently godly lives, taking part in the celebrations of the church. They find satisfaction in this double life, even as it harms the body.

The heart desires of false teachers comes out in their eyes. 'They have eyes full of adultery, insatiable for sin. They entice unsteady souls. They have hearts trained in greed' (2:14). The phrase, "eyes full of adultery," can be literally translated "having eyes full of an adulteress," like the pornography viewer today.[6] They are manipulative in their efforts to control others, especially the vulnerable, for their own ends. On Christ's behalf, Peter declares judgment: they are 'accursed children! Forsaking the right way, they have gone astray' (2:14–15).

Turning to the Old Testament, Peter tells us that the false teachers 'have followed the way of Balaam who was rebuked for his own transgression; a speechless donkey spoke with human voice and restrained the prophet's madness' (2:14–16). While holy angels do not bring accusations against false teachers, God can use animals, who do not even bear the image of God, to rebuke false teachers. The picture is clear: false teachers elevate themselves above the angels, but in reality are living below an animal level. They are the most disappointing emptiness in the fallen natural order: 'these are waterless springs and mists driven by a storm' (2:17). Initially, they appear to have promise "of doing much good to the church ... while in effect they but disappoint poor souls and darken the truth."[7] Their end is grim: 'For them the gloom of utter darkness has been reserved' (2:17). God's wrath is prepared for them, a fearful and radical contrast to the "living hope through the resurrection of Jesus Christ ... an inheritance that is imperishable, undefiled, and unfading, kept in heaven" for God's children (1 Peter 1:3–4).

Again, Peter speaks about the danger of false teachers. The seriousness of the threat merits multiple rememberings. The emphasis in verses 18 and 19 is on the false teacher's utter confidence, and their use of sexual and other passions to draw the spiritually weak and vulnerable to join with them. 'For speaking loud boasts of folly, they entice by sensual passions of the flesh those who are barely escaping from those who live in error. They promise them freedom, but they themselves are slaves of corruption. For whatever overcomes a person, to that he is enslaved' (2:18–19). Much like Satan, their father, they promise much—in this case the freedom to be yourself—but in reality they are "slaves of corruption" enslaving others to the same.

The final warning of this passage is addressed to both false teachers and those who would follow them away from Christ. 'For if, after they have escaped the defilements of the world through the knowledge of our Lord and Savior Jesus Christ, they are again entangled in them and overcome, the last state has become worse for them than the first' (2:20). These words should make us tremble at the thought of giving sin any place in our hearts and minds. They should make us run from every temptation straight to Christ. They should make us quick and earnest in repenting of the beginnings of sin. What could be more awful than to appear to come to Christ and gain deliverance from sin, but then over time prove the contrary? To have been so close to life in Christ, and yet to turn back to sin and death? The apostle soberly concludes 'it would have been better for them to have never known the way of righteousness than after knowing it to turn back from the holy commandment delivered to them. What the true proverb says has happened to them: "The dog returns to its own vomit, and the sow, after washing herself, returns to wallow in the mire"' (2:21–22).

You and the Word

These solemn warnings are the words of the ascended Christ to us. Our Lord Jesus is the Good Shepherd and Good Teacher. He saved and transformed Peter to love him, and to feed and tend the sheep—including us by warning us against false shepherds, thieves, and wolves (John 10:1–16). Our Lord faithfully shepherds and preserves his church through this world, partly by unmasking patterns of sin and evil. He is the faithful Savior, who also will never forsake us (Hebrews 13:5–6). Charles Spurgeon reflects

> These "false teachers" would deceive the very elect of God if it were possible, but they are not easily deceived, for God has given them a discerning mind by which they are to "try the spirits whether they are of God." The Lord Jesus said of His sheep, "A stranger they will not follow, but will flee from him: for they know not the voice of strangers." Sheep though they are, they have discernment enough to know their shepherd—and the godly soon detect false teachers ...[8]

How can you best guard yourself, your family, and your church from false teachers? How can you overcome the sin that remains within? By "looking to Jesus, the founder and perfecter of your faith" (Hebrews 12:2). Living in communion with him, loving to listen to his Word, and being filled with the rich truth of what he says is the best means to grow strong in overcoming sin, and being able to discern and escape the false teachers who rise up within the church. Jesus said, "My sheep hear my voice, and I know them, and they follow me. I give them eternal life, and they will never perish, and no one will snatch them out of my hand" (John 10:27–28).

> I love thy kingdom, Lord, the house of thine abode,
> The church our blest Redeemer saved with his own precious blood.
>
> I love they church, O God: her walls before thee stand,
> Dear as the apple of thine eye, and graven on thy hand.
>
> Jesus, thou friend divine, our Savior and our King,
> Thy hand from ev'ry snare and foe shall great deliverance bring.

Sure as thy truth shall last, to Zion shall be giv'n
The brightest glories earth can yield, and brighter bliss of heav'n.[9]

5

The Coming Day of the Lord

Please read 2 Peter 3:1–18

The Word of God is Certain (3:1–7)

Peter begins the third chapter of the epistle with tenderness: 'This is now the second letter that I am writing to you, beloved' (3:1). Even strong believers need the Word brought to them repeatedly. 'In both of them I am stirring up your sincere mind by way of reminder' (3:1). Our Lord knows we need steady encouragement, stirring up, and revival; he gives it by his Word and Spirit (Haggai 1:14; Psalm 85:6). The particular spiritual concern that Peter expresses here is our tendency to become focused on our present earthly existence, losing sight of Christ and his coming return in glory. The solution is 'that you should remember the predictions of the holy prophets and the commandment of the Lord and Savior through your apostles' (3:2). By remembering and meditating on the Bible's teaching and revelation of Christ, "the pure minds of Christians are to be stirred up, that they may be active and lively in the work of holiness, and zealous and unwearied in the way of heaven."[1]

Another reason that we need to be stirred up is because the world around us actively works to suppress any thought of the return of Christ, trying to pull us along. 'Knowing this first of all that scoffers will come in the last days with scoffing, following their own sinful desires' (3:2) Those in love with their sin will do everything to evade the reality of their accountability and coming judgment, including mocking it as though it were a myth. They will say, 'They will say, "Where is the promise of his coming? For ever since the fathers fell asleep, all things are continuing as they were from the beginning of creation"' (3:4). In Peter's day the apparent unchanging uniformity of human existence was extrapolated backwards to the ancient days and then forwards to push any thought of God far away—much as evolutionary theories do today.

But Peter, like Paul, notes that this is a suppression of the truth in unrighteousness (Romans 1:18–20). 'For they deliberately overlook this fact, that the heavens existed long ago, and the earth was formed out of water and through water by the Word of God' (3:5). There is an intentional ignoring of the fact that God is the One who by the sudden, supernatural power of his Word brought the universe, and the earth itself into existence, within the space of six days (Genesis 1:1–10). The fact that God subsequently, in history, used created waters in the flood of judgement on humanity (Genesis 6–9) is also omitted: 'and that by means of these the world that then existed was deluged with water and perished' (3:6). But by the same sovereign power exercised in creation and the flood, God sustains the created order of which the scoffers and ungodly are a part. 'By the same word the heavens and earth that now exist are stored up for fire, being kept until the day of judgement and destruction of the ungodly' (3:7). The present order is being kept by God with the coming purpose of judgement by fire in view: the day is coming when he will bring the rebellion of this world to a full stop. His Word is always faithful and true; his promises never fail.

The Day of the Lord Will Come (3:8–13)

The fact that thousands of years of human history have passed since the patriarchs, without a massive judgement, is no ground for spiritual complacency. Peter tells us 'but do not overlook this one fact, beloved, that with the Lord one day is as a thousand years, and a thousand years as one day' (3:8). God's ways are higher than our ways; he is the infinite, eternal, and unchanging God, we are his finite, time-bound creatures. The vast sweep of time he has created, as well as the most minute details of the passage of time are all within his power, perfect understanding, and plan: time is part of his creation. We are creatures of time, and he is the Creator and Sustainer of time.

God graciously shares with us why the significant passage of sinful human history before a holy God has, and still continues to occur. 'The Lord is not slow to fulfill his promise as some count slowness, but is patient towards you, not wishing that any should perish, but that all should reach repentance' (3:9). The ongoing passage of time prior to the final judgement is not because God is slack in judging sin; it is because in his great grace, love and mercy he is saving sinners from every generation, and from every tribe and tongue and nation under heaven (Revelation 7:9). Peter applies this directly to the church: the reason God's judgement has not yet come is because he is "patient toward you" (3:9). He wants you to reach repentance, turning to him and receiving new, eternal life with him through Jesus Christ.

But God's patience is not slackness. 'The day of the Lord will come like a thief, and then the heavens and earth will pass away with a roar, and the heavenly bodies will be burned up and dissolved, and the earth and the works that are done on it will be exposed' (3:10). The call to new life in Christ is urgent (3:10). Cataclysmic, inescapable, global judgment is coming: "God will bring every deed into judgement, with every secret thing, whether good or evil" (Ecclesiastes 12:14). The Lord Jesus will be "revealed from heaven with his mighty angels in flaming fire, inflicting vengeance on those who do not know God and on those who do not obey the gospel of our Lord Jesus ... when he comes on that day to be glorified in his saints" (2 Thessalonians 1:7–10). The present order is not endless.

Anticipation and Diligence (3:14–18)

Peter concludes the epistle with application. 'Therefore, beloved, since you are waiting for these, be diligent to be found by him without spot or blemish, and at peace' (3:14). Jesus' precious blood has been shed for us, as "a lamb without blemish or spot" (1 Peter 1:19). He is sufficient to cleanse, sustain in growing holiness, making us a holy contrast to the false teachers who are blots and blemishes. At the same time, in Christ we are responsible, able, and called to diligent pursuit of holistic life in Christ. Living life in Christ means being at peace with God—ready for his return. Peter repeats in verses 15 and 16 what he stated in verse 9, for the sake of those in the church, but also undoubtedly with a view to those outside (cf. Matthew 28:19–20; Mark 16:15; Acts 1:8). 'And count the patience of our Lord as salvation, just as our beloved brother Paul also wrote to you according to the wisdom given him, as he does in all his letters when he speaks in them of these matters' (3:15–16). Scripture's consistent statement is, "Today is the day of salvation" (Hebrews 3 and 4); Peter cites Paul's epistles to confirm this (2 Corinthians 6:2).

Even as Peter cites Paul's epistles, showing the unity of God's Word, he tells the church that the truths in these same epistles have been twisted by false teachers, and by untaught, unstable readers. 'There are some things in them that are hard to understand, which the ignorant and unstable twist to their own destruction, as they do the other Scriptures' (3:16). Our understanding will be challenged by the heights and depths of what God reveals to us in his Word. While this humbles the Christian to a careful study of the Word, it proves a stumbling block to those apart from Christ. 'You therefore, beloved, knowing this beforehand, take care that you are not carried away with the error of lawless people and lose your own stability' (3:17). Peter gives us the antidote to this danger—interpreting Scripture by Scripture, in reliance on the Lord (Psalm 36:9). Christ has promised "to guide us into all truth" by his Spirit, just as he did with the disciples on the road to Emmaus (John 16:13; Luke 24:32). Peter's epistles and Paul's epistles, are consistent and unified because the same Holy Spirit inspired them (2 Peter 1:21).

Peter concludes by calling the church to 'grow in the grace and knowledge of our Lord Jesus' (3:18). As we do we are "rooted and built up in him and established in the faith" (Colossians 2:6). He is our perfect Savior who restores us to glorify and enjoy him forever. Our only fitting response, like Peter, is to join in doxology: 'To him be the glory both now and to the day of eternity. Amen' (3:18).

You and the Word

Spiritual revival occurs through the recovery and diligent use of the ordinary means of grace (prayer, reading and preaching of the Word, and the sacraments) in communion with God in Christ. In the book of Nehemiah we see that men, women, and "all who could understand" became attentive to God's Word and were spiritually transformed. As they understood, they worshipped, wept, and rejoiced in the Lord (Nehemiah 8:1–18). They feasted together and were glad. Reading and studying 1 and

2 Peter is sharing in the same privilege as the covenant people under Nehemiah. We do so in far greater fullness, for Christ has come, made atonement, and is risen and ascended to glory. By faith, look forward to the coming day of his return when sin and evil will be brought to a complete end. "According to his promise we are waiting for new heavens and a new earth in which righteousness dwells" (2 Peter 3:13). As you anticipate the return of your Lord, continue to diligently pursue all that he calls you to.

Our God shall surely come, and silence shall not keep;
Before him fire shall waste, and storms tempestuous round him sweep.
He to the heav'ns above shall then send forth his call,
And likewise to the earth, that he may judge his people all.

Together let my saints unto me gathered be,
Those that by sacrifice have made a covenant with me.
Then shall the heavens declare his righteousness abroad;
Because the Lord himself is judge, yea, none is judge but God.[2]

Notes

An Introduction to the Epistles of Peter

1. "Apostle" in Colin Brown, ed., *New International Dictionary of New Testament Theology*, vol. 1 (Grand Rapids: Zondervan, 1986), 126–137.

2. Where the ESV translates the description of the recipients as "elect exiles of the dispersion" other translations render the description as "scattered strangers or aliens" leaving the term "elect" to be translated as such in the beginning of verse two, as such more closely following the pattern of the Greek.

3. Though some recent scholars, such as Richard Bauckham, have sought to argue against Peter's direct authorship of the epistle, they have been unable to marshal compelling support for their case, as Simon Kistemaker notes. Simon Kistemaker, *New Testament Commentary: Peter and Jude* (Grand Rapids: Baker, 1993), 213–219, 322. See also D.A. Carson, Douglas Moo, and Leon Morris, *An Introduction to the New Testament* (Grand Rapids: Zondervan, 1992), 433–443, and Richard Bauckham, *Word Biblical Commentary: Jude, 2 Peter* (Waco, Texas: Word Books, 1983), 158–163.

4. Charles Simeon, *Expository Outlines on the Whole Bible*, vol. 20 (Grand Rapids: Baker, 1988), 130.

The First Epistle of Peter: Hope and Holiness (1 Peter 1–5)

Chapter 1 Sovereign Grace and Peace

1. The King James and New King James translations place the word elect at the beginning of verse 2; the English Standard Version and New International Version at this point more closely follow the Greek text, placing the word elect in verse 1.
2. Mark Webb, "What Difference Does It Make?" *Reformation and Revival Journal* vol. 3 (Winter 1994) 1:53–54.
3. Alexander Nisbet, *1 & 2 Peter* (Edinburgh: Banner of Truth, 1982), 9.
4. John Brown, *Expository Discourses on the First Epistle of the Apostle Peter* (Marsallton, Del: The National Foundation for Christian Education, n.d.), 20.
5. Brown, 22–23.
6. John Calvin, *Commentaries on the First Epistle of Peter* (Grand Rapids: Baker, 1981), 27.

Chapter 2 Sons of God

1. Calvin, 28.
2. J. Ramsey Michaels, *Word Biblical Commentary: 1 Peter* (Nashville: Thomas Nelson, 1988), 17.
3. The wording in the Greek text is: ἄφθαρτον καὶ ἀμίαντον καὶ ἀμάραντον.
4. "Heidelberg Catechism" in *Ecumenical creeds and reformed confessions* (Grand Rapids: CRC Publications, 1988), 13.

Chapter 3 The Testing of Your Faith

1. Edmund Clowney, *The Message of 1 Peter* (Downers Grove, IL: InterVarsity Press, 1988), 51.

2. Michaels, 35–36.

3. Brown, 77–78.

4. William Cowper, "God Moves in a Mysterious Way" in *Trinity Hymnal* (Suwanee, GA: Great Commission Publications, 1990), 128.

Chapter 4 Holy Anticipation

1. Jonathan Edwards, *The Religious Affections* (Carlisle, PA: Banner of Truth, 1994), 122.

2. Author unknown, "Be Thou My Vision" in *Trinity Hymnal* (Suwanee, GA: Great Commission Publications, 1990), 642.

Chapter 5 Holy Action

1. Robert Leighton, *Commentary on First Peter* (Grand Rapids: Kregel, 1972), 76.

2. John Owen, *Of the Mortification of Sin in Believers* in William H. Goold, ed., *The Works of John Owen* vol. 6 (Edinburgh: The Banner of Truth, 1977), 9.

Chapter 6 Holy Fear and Trusting Faith

1. Leighton, 84.

2. Leighton, 85.

3. John Murray, *Redemption Accomplished and Applied* (Grand Rapids: Eerdmans, 1955), 25.

4. Isaac Watts, "When I Survey the Wondrous Cross" in *Trinity Hymnal* (Suwanee, GA: Great Commission Publications, 1990), 252.

Chapter 7 The Eternal Word and Christian Love

1. Oxford Dictionaries, www.oxforddictionaries.com. Accessed 22 March 2016.

2. Brown, 193.

3. Ralph Wardlaw, "Christ of All My Hopes the Ground", in *Trinity Hymnal* (Suwanee, GA: Great Commission Publications, 1990), 518.

Chapter 8 Like Living Stones

1. Matthew Henry, *Commentary on the Whole Bible* (Peabody, MA: Hendrikson, 1994), 6:818.

2. Both Peter and Paul cite a commonly available Greek translation of the Old Testament, part of a family of early New Testament era translations of the Hebrew text known as the Septuagint.

3. Horatius Bonar, "Fill Thou My Life, O Lord My God" in *Trinity Hymnal* (Suwanee, GA: Great Commission Publications, 1990), 589.

Chapter 9 Proclaiming the Excellencies of God

1. "The wonder is that God chooses any. Certainly God does not choose an elite. Israel is a chosen people, but not a choice people." Clowney, 91.

2. Clowney, 95.

Chapter 10 Abstaining and Excelling

1. John Bunyan, *The Holy War* (North Kensington, PA: Whitaker House, 1985).

2. Isaac Watts, "What Shall I Render to My God" in *Trinity Hymnal* (Suwanee, GA: Great Commission Publications, 1990), 637.

Chapter 12 Following in Jesus' Steps

1. Kate B. Wilkinson, "May the Mind of Christ My Savior" in *Trinity Hymnal* (Suwanee, GA: Great Commission Publications, 1990), 644.

Chapter 14 God's Calling for All of Us

1. Calvin, 102–103.

2. Keith Getty and Stewart Townend, "O Church Arise" (Nashville, TN: Getty Music, 2016).

Chapter 16 Encouragements to Faithfulness

1. R. C. H. Lenski, *The Interpretation of The Epistles of St. Peter, St. John and St. Jude* (Columbus, Ohio: Wartburg Press, 1945), 155.

Chapter 17 United to Christ, Living for God

1. Michaels, 234.
2. C.H. Spurgeon, *Commentary on 1 & 2 Peter and Jude* (Titus Books, 2014). Kindle edition.
3. Clowney, 178.
4. Calvin, 131.
5. Calvin, 131.
6. Samuel J. Stone, "The Church's One Foundation" in *Trinity Hymnal* (Suwanee, GA: Great Commission Publications, 1990), 347.

Chapter 18 Sharing in Christ's Sufferings

1. Spurgeon, Kindle edition.
2. Dwight F. Zeller, *1 Peter: An exegetical procedure which explores the Epistle of 1 Peter* (Westcliffe, Colorado: Sangre de Cristo Seminary, 2009), 211.
3. Calvin, 139.
4. John MacArthur, *1 & 2 Peter: Courage in Times of Trouble* (Nashville: Thomas Nelson, 2006), 47.
5. Spurgeon, Kindle edition.
6. Thomas Kelly, "The Head that once was crowned with thorns" in *Trinity Hymnal* (Suwanee, GA: Great Commission Publications, 1990), 298.

Chapter 19 Shepherd the Flock

1. Spurgeon, Kindle edition.
2. 1 Peter 5:2, King James Version.
3. Spurgeon, Kindle edition.
4. Francis Havergal, "Take My Life and Let It Be" (1874)

Chapter 20 The Perseverance of the Church

1. Henry, 6:833.
2. Translated as "the church that is at Babylon" in the Geneva Bible and the King James Version.

The Second Epistle of Peter: Truth and Triumph (2 Peter 1–3)

Chapter 1 The God Who Gives

1. δοῦλος. See "slave" in Colin Brown, ed., *The New International Dictionary of New Testament Theology* (Grand Rapids: Zondervan, 1986), 3:592–598.
2. Nisbet, 224.
3. John Calvin, *Commentaries on the Second Epistle of Peter* (Grand Rapids: Baker, 1981), 369.
4. Simon Kistemaker, *New Testament Commentary: Exposition of the Epistles of Peter and of the Epistles of Jude* (Grand Rapids: Baker, 1987), 248.
5. Nisbet, 226.
6. Charles Wesley, "And Can It Be That I Should Gain" in *Trinity Hymnal* (Suwanee, GA: Great Commission Publications, 1990), 455.
7. C.H. Spurgeon, *The Immutability of God: A Sermon Delivered on Sabbath Morning, January 7th, 1855.*

Chapter 2 A Useful, Fruitful Life

1. Calvin, 373.
2. Nisbet, 227.
3. Jerry Bridges, *The Practice of Godliness* (Colorado Springs, CO: NavPress, 2008).
4. R.C.H. Lenski, *The Interpretation of the Epistles of St. Peter, St. John and St. Jude* (Columbus, OH: Wartburg Press, 2008) 269.
5. Calvin, 374.
6. Henry, 6:839.

Chapter 3 Why We Obey the Word

1. Calvin, 382.

Chapter 4 False Teachers Among You

1. Nisbet, 246.
2. Thomas Schreiner, *The New American Commentary: 1, 2 Peter, Jude* (Nashville, TN: Broadman & Holman, 2003), 332.
3. Henry, 843.
4. Calvin, 400.
5. Lenski, 318–319.
6. Lenski, 324.
7. Nisbet, 267.
8. Spurgeon, Kindle edition.
9. Timothy Dwight, "I Love Thy Kingdom, Lord" in *Trinity Hymnal* (Suwanee, GA: Great Commission Publications, 1990), 353.

Chapter 5 The Coming Day of the Lord

1. Henry, 847.

2. Psalm 50:1–6, "The Mighty God the Lord" in in *Trinity Hymnal* (Suwanee, GA: Great Commission Publications, 1990), 455.